Where You Become True Is The Place Of Truth

Human completion is returning to the original foundation - the source of the world.

A person reborn in the original foundation while he is living is

a complete person who lives forever.

Where You Become True Is
The Place Of Truth
by Woo Myung

First Edition
First Printing Jul. 2012
Second Printing Jan. 2013

Published by Cham Books
1202 Kifer Rd., Sunnyvale, CA 94086, USA
Tel: (408) 475-8783
contact@chambooks.com
www.chambooks.com

ISBN: 978-0-9849124-1-4

Library of Congress Control Number: 2012941901

This book has been translated into English
from the original Korean text published in Aug. 2008.
Translated by members of the Maum Meditation Translation Team.

Book Design by Color of Dream

Printed in Seoul, Korea

Where You Become True Is The Place Of Truth

Woo Myung

Woo Myung, bestselling author of many books about Truth, attained enlightenment after deep introspection about life and existence. When he became Truth, he dedicated his life to teaching others to become Truth and founded Maum Meditation. For his efforts, he was awarded the Mahatma Gandhi Peace Award by the United Nations International Association of Educators for World Peace (IAEWP) in September 2002. Woo Myung has also been appointed as a United Nations World Peace Ambassador.

He is the author of numerous books including *World Beyond World*, *The Way To Become A Person In Heaven While Living*, *Nature's Flow* and *Stop Living In This Land, Go To The Everlasting World Of Happiness, Live There Forever* which have been published in English. His other books, *Heaven's Formula For Saving The World*, *The Living Eternal World*, *The Book Of Wisdom*, *Mind*, and *The Enlightened World* are in the process of being translated into English as well as Japanese, Chinese, French, Italian, Spanish, Portuguese, German and Swedish.

Contents

• Preface 10

Part 1

• The Human Mind 15 • Truth And Falseness I 18 • Heaven And Hell 20 • A Person Can Go To Heaven Only When He Becomes Truth While He Is Living 22 • Only Truth Can Make Truth 24 • Huh, Huh, Cham (False, False, Truth) 26 • Salvation Is Falseness Being Made To Become Truth 27 • What Is The Master Of The Universe? 29 • Does One Live Eternally With The Body Or With The Mind? 31 • All That Have Not Become Truth Are False 33 • Falseness And Truth 35 • Only Christ Is Truth 37 • The Complete World 39 • Those Who Are Unable To Complete The Meditation 40 • What Is Salvation? It Is Falseness Becoming Truth 42 • The Way Forward For Mankind 44 • What Is The End Of The World? 46 • True Wisdom 49 • Man Does Not Know Anything And All Of His Words And Actions Are False 52 • Nothing Is Right In Man's World 54 • Sins Committed In The Mind Are Sins 56 • Man Is A Ghost 58 • For The World To Become Complete 60 • Do You Know Where You Will Go After You Die? 61 • What Is Samsara (The Eternal Cycle Of Birth, Death And Rebirth)? 64 • The False Mind, The Original Mind 65 • How Can One Know Truth? 66 • Do Heaven And Hell Truly Exist? 68 • Going To The Complete World While Living 70 • The True Meaning Behind "The Faithful Will Go To Heaven" 72 • What Is Real (Truth), What is Fake (Falseness) 73 • One Can Go To Heaven Only When He Has Completely Eliminated His Sins And Karma 75 • Only Truth Can Make One Become Truth 76 • What Is Wisdom? 78 • Truth Remains Once All Falseness Have Been Destroyed 80 • Why Man Needs To Be Saved 81

Part 2

• *Dō* Is The Ordinary 87 • The World Is As You See It, Just As It Exists 89 • From Negativity To Positivity 91 • From Non-existence To Existence 93 • What Exists In the World Exists, And What Does Not Exist In The World Does Not Exist 95 • To Be Reborn Or Resurrected, One Must First Die 97 • Man's Sin 98 • Those Who Have Sold Out Their True Souls 100 • A Complete Person 102 • What Man Needs To Achieve And Do 104 • Chundo (Prayers Or Rites For The Passage Of The Dead Into Heaven) 106 • Many People Ask If Maum Meditation Is A Religion 107 • The Way Forward For Man 109 • The Reason Man Is False 111 • Maum Meditation Makes That Which Does Not Exist In The World Exist 112 • What Is Life? 115 • Resurrection 117 • To Be Holy Or Divine 120 • The Meaning Of A High Level Of *Dō* 121 • The Savior 122 • The Age Of Addition 123 • Not Even The Affairs Of The Human World Can Be Successfully Achieved With The Human Mind 125 • The Work Of Maum Meditation 127

Part 3
Poems

• The Frailty Of Human Life 133 • A Picture 135 • Nature's Flow 138 • Truth And Falseness II 141 • Ignorant Of Truth's Will 143 • A Limited Time 144 • A Virtuous Person Has Nowhere In The World To Rest 147 • Maum Meditation Is About Discarding Everything, Not Having More 151 • The Past, Present And Future, Good, Bad, Burdens And Sufferings Exist In the False Ghost World Where Man Lives, But None Of These Things Exist In God's World 153 • When Will The Messiah Come? 155 • The Reason Man Cannot See Truth Or Know Truth 157 • Enlightenment 159 • A Lifetime 160 • The Non-Existent World 162 • Come Out Into The World 164 • If It Is Not Truth And Real, It Is False 166 • The Meaningless Stories Of Life 169 • A Life Of Nature's Flow 173 • There Is No Truth In Human Conceptions And Habits 176 • The Living World 178 • The Reason Man Cannot Live Like Flowing Water 179 • The World Of Divine Beings 181 • Let's Work In The New World And Amass Blessings 183

Part 4
Poems

• The Way To Be Born In Heaven And Live There 189 • Man's Fate Inside His Baggage 191 • The Providence Of Nature 193 • Those Illusions…. 195 • One Must Be The Origin In Order To Live As The True Origin 198 • A Divine Being Just Lives 200 • The Reason And Purpose All Creations Were Born Is To Become Reborn As The Body And Mind Of This Existence And Live Forever 203 • The Complete Land 205 • Untitled 1 207 • Untitled 2 208 • Heaven, Which Is Truth 210 • *Haewonsangsaeng* - Living In Harmony Free From Bitterness And Regrets 215 • A Poem Of The World 221 • The Illusionary Affairs of Human Life 224 • The Life Truth Leads When It Is Born In The World 227 • The Mountains, Streams And Nature Are Alive 230 • He Who Is Born In Heaven Lives In Heaven While He Who Is Born On Earth Lives On Earth 234 • He Who Has Become A Proper Person Will Teach Properly And Live Properly 236 • One's Life After He Has Become Real 241 • The Best Way To Do Maum Meditation 245 • The Savior, Maitreya, And *Jung-do-ryung* Is The Person Who Creates Things That Are Real 246 • The Age Of Man I 248 • The Mind Of The Origin 250 • We Must Come Out From The Shadows, The Illusions, Into The World 253 • The Land Of God Where Time Does Not Exist 255 • A Life Lived By Truth 258

Part 5
Poems

• The Age Of Man II 265 • Spring, Summer, Fall and Winter 271 • Let's Become True People 275 • The True World 280 • An Immigrant Must Go To The Place Where He Can Become Truth, Man Must Go To The Place Where He Can Become Truth 282 • *Ulleung* Island 286 • A True Person Lives A True Life 289 • God Is Complete And Lives Forever - God Is A Person Who Does Not Have A False Self And Has Been Reborn As God 290 • Illusion And Reality 294 • Human Completion 296 • The Hungered Affairs of Human Life 298 • Truth, Which Just Exists 299 • When I Began To Teach People 301 • Man's Destiny 305 • Let's Live A Lifetime Of The World 308 • Man Lives According To What He Has In His Mind 311 • It Is Okay For A Ghost To Have Nothing 315 • God 317 • Let's Go, Let's Go 319 • The Land Of Human Completion 321 • A Person Who Has Not Prepared Himself For Where He Needs To Go 324 • Acceptance 326 • Words That Are Of Use 327 • The Mind of Universal Order 328 • Let's Return To Nature 329 • In Order To Go To The True World 332 • The Principles Of The True World 335

Confirmation Questions - *Koans* 339

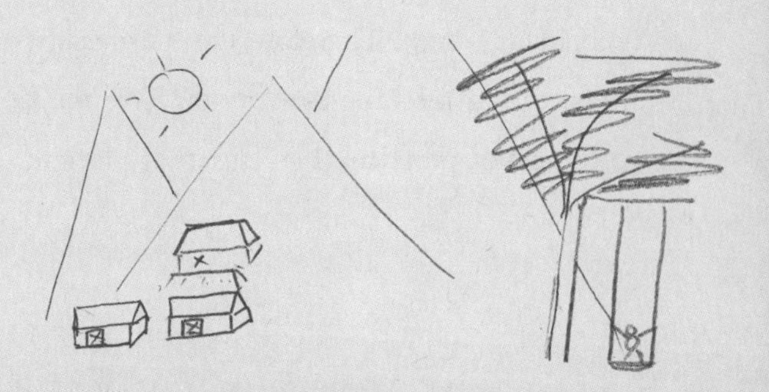

People have never known, not once in the many innumerable ages, what is true and what is false. What is true is the existence that is eternal and indestructible; the living existence that is the Universe itself; or in other words, this world. What is false is the human mind world, which is formed by taking pictures of the world in one's mind.

Man is living in this false world. He must therefore come out from his mind that is false, and be born in the world of Truth. If he does so, he will become complete and it will set right all religions, philosophies, ideologies and learning. It is then that man will be able to live happily and well.

Man does not know Truth and he has not been able to become Truth because having lived in a false world, he has only learned false things. This is the reason everyone lives with suffering and burden.

Truth knows what is true, as well as what is false; falseness lives in ignorance of both. Therefore the consciousness of a false person is dead. If you cannot become true or you have not become true at the place of your faith or practice, then isn't that place false?

Only a place where you are becoming true, a place where you can become true, is the true place. Human completion is to live resurrected in the true world after the false world and one's self living in it are completely gone. That time has now come, but people live unaware of Truth because their consciousnesses are so bound by their conceptions and habits. They are dead, but they live without knowing that they are.

The way for everyone to escape from the false world that is a dream and become Truth has now come to the world. I wrote this book in the hopes that it will help all people to become Truth and be reborn in the new complete world while they are living.

Woo Myung

Part 1

The real world is already complete, it is already enlightened.

Only man is dead for he lives in a world of pictures.

The Human Mind

Christianity tells us we have original and actual sin, and Buddhism tells us everything is in our minds and that what we hold in our minds is karma.

All religions tell us to cleanse and empty our minds, but this is often misunderstood. People commonly think that what is meant by this is to abandon or give up what they intended to do.

The human mind is the way one is living at present.

In Korea, there is a saying that you live according to what you have in your mind - according to the minds that you have "eaten". When we eat, the nutrients we need remain in our bodies, and what is not needed is excreted. The mind is what one has been born into, and in much the same way as food, the collective learning and experiences one takes in from birth. These things become one's "self" and dictate how he lives, which is why it is said that you live according to the minds you have eaten.

The experiences of your life become the foundation on which your individual mind is formed.

The human mind is like a video. This means man lives his life in an illusion from birth. It is comparable to a video because with his eyes, ears, nose, mouth and body - his five senses - he takes pictures of all that he experiences as he lives, and stores them inside him. These become his "self" and they dictate how he lives and behaves.

As man lives out his life within this mind - this "film" - he takes pictures of his hometown, his elementary, middle and high schools, college, military service, marriage, career and religious life; not only has he taken pictures in his mind of his entire past, but he will continue to do so even in the future of all that he sees, hears, speaks, smells and feels.

For example, anyone who has been to *Miami* Beach will have an image of Miami in his mind. Man's mind is exactly the same as a camera - the images on film in the camera are not real; they are false. The actual Miami Beach is what is real. What is inside the mind is false - they are like images on a reel of film.

It is because man is living inside a video that all religions tell us to cleanse and empty our minds; it is why we are told that the blessed are the poor in spirit for the kingdom of heaven is theirs. Man has always lived inside this mind, this film, and he has never once seen or lived in the complete world. This is what sin is; what karma is.

Your whole life, including everything that happened today, was simultaneously taken as a picture the moment you saw it. Moreover you are inside that film, the picture. When you think carefully about your day today, wasn't it all inside your mind?

We can live as one with the complete world when we destroy this picture world and come out from within it. We can become complete when we are resurrected after becoming one with the world created by the Creator who is complete. Thus, the mind that we must cleanse and empty is the world of pictures.

The real world is already complete; and it is already enlightened.

Only man is dead for he lives in a picture world. Man's mind is a mind world that is like a self-made video - a false world and an illusion. When seen from the real world, it is non-existent and when a person who is within this mind world dies, he disappears forever. However, man believes he is living in the actual world because his mind world overlaps the real world.

Man is not complete because he lives in a human mind world of the life that he has lived - a mind world constructed from pictures that were taken of the real world. This is the reason people seek religions and spiritual places - the reason they practice Maum Meditation. Man and his mind world are false.

Truth And Falseness I

I have asked people if they know what is true. I have also asked them if they know what is false.

No one has been able to give a proper answer to either question.

Truth is an existence that is real, everlasting, never-changing and alive. This existence is the sky before the sky - the Creator and the source of everything in heaven and earth.

The sky is the Creator and Truth itself which existed an eternity before and which will exist an eternity after. The stars, the sun, the moon and the Earth came from this sky as did people and everything on Earth. The sky is the source - everything came from it and therefore everything is the sky.

When the sky that is the Creator created all things, everything was made to live eternally; they were made to live to the age of the sky itself. However, man is unable to become Truth because of his sins and karma. He is false and therefore, dead. This is the reason Christianity tells us man will be saved at the second coming of Christ and Buddhism tells us that *Maitreya* will come to save the people of the world. Truth is the world: it is already complete, and it is an enlightened perfect existence.

When one sees from the perspective of the world - the great Universe - the world is perfection itself. Even though the world is enlightened, man is not complete because he is not living in the world. He merely thinks he is living in the world but instead, he is living in his own mind world - an illusionary world. Consequently he is not complete and needs salvation.

The world man lives in is an illusion because it is a world of his mind. This world is like a video and it overlaps the real world.

The human mind world is a world that has duplicated the real world, through the pictures he took with his eyes, and all that he has heard, smelled and felt. These have become his "self" and he lives within it, but seen from the real world, it is illusionary and it does not exist.

Truth is the world and falseness is man who lives within his mind world which has copied the world of Truth. Therefore, man must cleanse and discard his mind. He must become "poor in spirit" in order to go to the real world that is heaven.

Heaven And Hell

People often speak of going to heaven or hell after death. But what are heaven and hell? What happens to people after they die? Clear answers to these questions cannot be found anywhere; nowhere can one actually be enlightened of the answers.

The existence of the Creator is the great Universe itself. The great Universe originally created a complete world, and everything in the world is also already complete and living in heaven - the land of God.

From the perspective of the Universe that is the Creator, everything is the existence of Truth that is already enlightened and alive.

This existence of Truth in the world consists of a great Soul and Spirit - this is the metaphysical real substance and the master of the Universe. This existence is not material; it is the metaphysical real substance of Truth. It *is* Truth, which existed before the beginning and which will exist for eternity.

If you become one with this existence in the world of this existence, this place is heaven.

No one, not a single person, is able to go to heaven because of his sins and karma. From our childhoods until the present, we have each made a world of our own minds by copying the world. This world is hell. Man does not live in the world that is true, instead he makes and lives in his own false mind world. When one has such a world only what is in that world exists for him, so when he dies he dies forever within it.

This mind world does not exist from the viewpoint of the true world, but it exists for the person who is living in it. This illusionary world is like a dream - just as a dream no longer exists once you wake up, the illusionary world does not exist although it may seem to exist. Hence, it is hell. Man has no choice but to go to this world of hell after death because he is not born in the world that is true.

Man can be born in the world if he repents all of his sins; he can be reborn in the true world if his illusionary world no longer exists.

Heaven is a land where those who have become one with the world live. Hell is a non-existent illusionary world which is made of pictures of the world.

A person who has become one with the real world, and who has been born in the world while he is living, will live forever.

A Person Can Go To Heaven Only When He Becomes Truth While He Is Living

Through religion, we have gained the common belief that we will go to heaven after we die while people who do "bad" things will go to hell. However no one knows where heaven or hell is. To put it simply, heaven is the world where Truth - that which is real - lives and hell is false, a delusion, a non-existent world.

The fact that we were born into this world as human-beings is a miracle among miracles. We would not have been born if our parents and ancestors did not each in turn happen to conceive on the particular days and times that they did. And even then, we would not have been born if those eggs had been fertilized by one of the other millions and millions of sperm. Isn't our birth therefore a miracle? We were not born on the earth through this miracle, against such odds, only to live to the end of our life spans and die.

There must be a method, a way, to live eternally. Man must become Truth because there is no other way for him to live forever. Truth is what is real, what is true; and man cannot live without becoming Truth.

Doesn't it go against reason that someone who has not become true while he is living, that is, someone who has not been born in heaven while living, can go to heaven after he dies?

If you are to become Truth - attain human completion while you are living - your entire self which is false must disappear. Then, you can become Truth.

What is true is the world and what is false is one's self. Thus, if one eliminates his self completely, then what is true will emerge.

Only he who has been resurrected as Truth while he is living is true, and such a person will live in heaven, the land of Truth, forever.

He who dies as his false self will remain false, and what is false does not exist.

Only Truth Can Make Truth

What is Truth? Truth is the place of the everlasting, never-changing Universe before any creations came into existence. This place is the origin of Truth. In other words, the place where there is absolutely nothing in the Universe is the mother and father of all creations, and this existence is the origin of all creations. This existence is the original appearance of the everlasting and never-changing Truth.

All creations are the embodiment of this existence, so therefore all creations are also Truth. Man however, is false because he has turned his back on this existence and he lives within illusionary pictures of the shapes and forms of this existence that he has taken. It is because of this that he cannot see the living Truth, or see or hear the will of Truth. Therefore he does not know Truth.

The main point in the Bible is that there will be a second coming of Christ for the salvation of mankind. Only Jesus Christ is one with God, who is the existence of Truth. The term *Jesus* in Christianity refers to the existence of Truth. When it is said that only Jesus can give us salvation, it means only this existence of Truth can save us. Because man is trapped inside his sins, he is not able to see Truth even when

Truth is present. This is why it is also said that the Messiah, Jesus, will come like a thief in the night.

A person who has not become Truth cannot see Truth, even when Truth is present in the world. Only a person who has been born in the world of Truth can know Truth. Many Christians believe the Messiah will come with the same appearance as Jesus of two thousand years ago - I wish that people would recognize the existence of Truth that comes to the world, no matter what appearance he has.

Buddhism also tells us that *Maitreya* will come to the world to save the people of the world. Although the term used is different from the Christian one, it has the same meaning - it also refers to the existence of Truth. In other words, only when the master of the Universe before the Universe comes, can man be born as this existence of Truth. And only this existence can make man who is false into a true person.

Truth is the great Universe itself. The *Jung* and *Shin*, that is, the Soul and Spirit, the body and mind, the Holy Spirit and Holy Father, *Dharmakaya* and *Sambhogakaya* of the great Universe must come as a human-being in order to teach mankind and save them.

There must be Truth in order for one to become Truth. Only the existence of Truth can enable man who is false to be born as Truth.

To produce sesame, you must have sesame seeds. The reason mankind has yet to become complete is the same as why you cannot produce sesame without sesame seeds.

Only the existence of Truth can make Truth. Therefore this existence will teach Truth so people can become Truth.

Huh, Huh, Cham
(False, False, Truth)

Man lives in a world of sentient beings; a *saha* world; a world of hell; a world of sin and karma.

Man mistakenly believes he lives in the world but he does not. He lives in a world made by his own mind so he cannot become one with the world. The world he lives in is a world of sin and karma, a *saha* world, and a world of hell because he lives trapped inside a world of his own mind.

This world that he has made is a false, non-existent world. Because it is false, it disappears when you get rid of it - it is an illusionary world. When you eliminate this falseness repeatedly, Truth will remain.

Truth that remains once you have destroyed all falseness does not disappear however much you try to destroy it. This is the meaning behind the Korean saying, "*Huh, huh, cham*".

Salvation Is Falseness Being Made To Become Truth

When the Messiah comes to the world he will chase out all demons from the world of sin and take man to heaven.

What is man's sin?

Man's sin is turning his back on the world that is Truth, God, Christ and the great Universe, and trying to make the world his. He does this by making a false world through the pictures he takes in his mind, until his death.

Our very selves are illusions and we are ghosts from the moment we are born because our ancestors also lived in a false world of sin. This is called original sin. The *saha* world - the world of sentient beings - is also an illusion.

Even though man lives in a picture, a photo, formed from the images he has taken with his eyes, nose and ears from childhood, he believes he lives in the real world.

If you want evidence that you live inside a picture, think of everything that you did this morning: isn't it all inside your mind?

Isn't your whole life inside your mind also? Didn't you store all that you have seen, heard, smelled and felt in the world as pictures inside your mind?

The moment you look at the world, you take a picture and live in it. That picture is false and your self that lives in that picture is also false. We must escape from this false world - the world of sin, the *saha* world, the world of sentient beings or *sattvas* - and come out into the true world. This is salvation.

Salvation is falseness becoming true.

Salvation is when from the world of sin one is resurrected in the true world where there are no sins. It is escaping from the *saha* world. Man lives in a false world, therefore salvation is enabling him to live in the true world.

Salvation is falseness being made to become Truth.

What Is The Master Of The Universe?

In Buddhism the master of the Universe is called Buddha, while it is called God in Christianity. In Korea that is originally of the *Haneol-nim* ideology it is called *Haneol-nim*.

In any case, this existence - the master of the Universe - must be omnipotent and omniscient, the Creator and the existence of Truth. The existence that remains when you eliminate all creations from the Universe is the origin of all creation - this existence is the master, the Creator, and the original form and shape of the true existence.

This existence has a body and mind, thus the bodies and minds of all creation are representations of this existence. The body and mind of this existence is called *Dharmakaya* and *Sambhogakaya*, Holy Spirit and Holy Father, and also *Jung* and *Shin*.

This existence is a metaphysical real existence; it is the living Truth; and it is the omnipotent and omniscient existence itself. This existence is the mother and father of all things, the origin, the source, and the master. This existence existed before the beginning of all things and it will exist after the end. It is a complete existence that exists of and by itself.

This existence exists everywhere in the Universe regardless of time and space, and all creations were created by this existence.

Man cannot see this existence because it is not material. It can only be known when his mind, his consciousness, returns to it by destroying all of his conceptions and habits. While living in the world, we are able to distinguish between what is true and false to the extent of what we have in our minds. In the same way, this existence must be inside one's mind in order to know it. Thus when one destroys the world of his conceptions he is able to know this existence that is true, for it then exists inside his mind.

This existence is Truth that is eternal, never-changing and alive. Even when all creations in the Universe disappear, this existence exists as it is. It is not material; it is a metaphysical real existence. The only Truth is this existence and there is no way to live other than to be reborn as this existence. When you are resurrected after becoming one with this existence, you will live in the land of this existence as an immortal.

The origin of all things is the place where all things have been eliminated from the Universe and all things that exist are also this existence itself. It is this Soul and Spirit that lives forever. Therefore, man will be able to live forever if he is reborn as the body and mind of this existence itself.

Does One Live Eternally With The Body Or With The Mind?

Some sects of Christianity assert that a person who is the omnipotent and omniscient God will live for eternity in the world with his human body. They also argue that the Bible makes the same claim.

But nothing material in the world lasts forever. Even now, there are stars in the sky that are disappearing and new ones being created. Stars, which have the longest lifespan of any creation in the Universe, live for approximately five to fourteen billion years. The Earth is a star, as are the moon and sun. Therefore, the Earth will also someday disappear.

Has anyone seen a person live forever? Has anyone seen an animal live forever? The fact that nature and all creations change and disappear is Truth.

The way for the forms of all creations born in the world to live forever is to be resurrected as the body and mind of the Universe that is Truth. Only then can their Souls and Spirits live forever in the land of the Universe's true existence. The fact that the body disappears is Truth, and only the Universe's body and mind that has become Truth can live eternally.

Only he who is resurrected as the Soul and Spirit of the Creator - the metaphysical real substance - can live forever. Only he, who has become one with Truth in the land of Truth that is the non-material real existence, is Truth and is thus able to live forever.

Only the Soul and Spirit of Truth can live eternally.

All That Have Not Become Truth Are False

There is no one who knows what is true and what is false.

What is true is the eternally living existence of Truth. This existence is God, *Haneol-nim*, Buddha, Allah and the Creator. Even if the whole Universe disappears, doesn't the sky in the sky still exist? Even though everything is the empty sky, within the empty sky the one God exists. This empty existence is the Universe's body that created all creations. God is the mind of all creations. This body and mind are Truth and there is no way to live forever without becoming one with this existence that is true.

Man's mind is a mind that duplicates the world and man lives inside this copied mind. This is the reason religions ask us to empty and cleanse our minds.

It is common sense that one cannot live unless he is resurrected or reborn as Truth while he is living. If one is not true while he is living, if he is not Truth *now*, then isn't he false? If falseness dies it will die forever because it is false. If one is to become true, his false self needs to die completely. He can then be resurrected as Truth.

Being reborn or resurrected can happen only when falseness is completely dead. One cannot be reborn or resurrected if his false self still remains.

Only he who has achieved Truth, human completion, while he is living can live forever.

Only a person who has become one with the eternally living, never-changing Truth while he is living *is* Truth reborn. Therefore, only such a person does not die.

It is common sense that only those who become Truth while they are living can live forever.

If one dies, it is an eternal death because a person who is false does not exist.

Falseness And Truth

People insist their own religions are right and that other religions are cults or heretical.

Falseness is always false even if it appears similar to Truth and it is false even if it speaks of Truth. Truth must *be* Truth for it to be true.

While travelling around the world, I have seen a lot of in-fighting in each religion - they seem to lack wisdom. Then, what exactly is Truth? If you have not become Truth, that is real and true, aren't you false? Have you become complete? And if you have not, then again, aren't you false?

The way for falseness to become Truth is to discard one's false body and mind entirely.

Only a person who eliminates all of his self, just as Christ did by being crucified, can become Truth. Buddhism speaks of a "big" death, *mahanirvana*, a death without remains, *paranirvana*, and a perfect death, *nistha nirvana*. If one dies in such a "big" way and eliminates all of one's false self without anything remaining, he will be resurrected because his sins and karma no longer exist.

Salvation is falseness becoming Truth. The way to become Truth is to discard one's false self; then only Truth will remain and he can be reborn as Truth.

Places which were unable to teach you how to become Truth now, or places which until now have not helped you to become Truth, are all false. Even if a place speaks of Truth and is similar to Truth, it is false if one cannot become Truth there.

If you are not complete, then aren't you false? This is a question that should be considered seriously.

Even if one memorizes the Buddhist scriptures, the Bible, the Koran, the Vedas or all the other scriptures in the world, Truth does not exist in what one has memorized. Truth emerges only when one repents all of his sins, and only then can he truly know the principles of Truth.

Only Christ Is Truth

Christianity tells us Christ is the son of God and that he is God himself. This is perfectly correct. It also says that Christ is the Way, the Truth, and Life, and that no one can go to heaven without going through him. This is also correct.

Because Christ is the Truth, the way to Truth is not only a path that we must all travel, it is also Truth, and true life. It is also correct that no one can go to heaven unless one becomes Christ who is Truth - no one can go to heaven without becoming Truth.

The existence of Christ is the incarnation of the Holy Father and Holy Spirit that is the Creator of the Universe. The Holy Father, Holy Spirit and Holy Son are one. If one is not resurrected as the Creator's body and mind just as Christ was - if one is not resurrected as the Holy Spirit and Holy Father that is Truth - he cannot become Truth. When it is said one must believe in Christ in order to go to heaven, it means that we must believe in Truth that is Christ.

There are many people who have an image of Christ in their minds and believe that means they have faith in Christ.

To go to heaven, believing in Truth is everything. Only when one becomes Truth can one go to heaven, and only Truth can live in the eternal kingdom. Instead of just knowing these words, one must become Truth that is one with Christ. Only he who has become so will live in the land of God forever.

Only Christ is true.

Only Christ is Truth.

Finally, the word *Christ* is another word for Truth. It will be possible to interpret the Bible correctly if one understands the word *Christ* as *Truth.*

The Complete World

To be complete is to be without death, and the world that lives eternally is the complete world.

When man has been resurrected with the mind of great nature, the world will become one and complete. In other words, only when man is reborn with the mind of God, the mind of the Universe, the distinction or separation between *you* and *me* will disappear. Then everybody can become one and live without death as Truth. Only then, is the world complete.

It is only possible to escape from the conditions of sickness, ageing, life and death when one's self that is an illusion has disappeared. The world is complete, but man is not able to become one with the world because of his mind; he is not complete because he has his own mind.

The world is already perfect, enlightened, and complete.

If man's mind is made to become one with the great Universe that is God, he will be resurrected in the true world - this is the complete world.

Those Who Are Unable To Complete The Meditation

In the early days of Maum Meditation, there were many people who came because they wanted to achieve Truth in order to become a superior version of themselves.

The path to becoming a saint is truly a long one. It is not easy to become a Buddha; it is not easy to become Truth.

Because man lives inside his mind, his own mind world, he needs to discard both his mind world and his self for Truth to emerge. When only Truth remains, he will become Truth. But this is difficult and many people give up along the way because instead of throwing away their selves and mind worlds, their false selves try to achieve Truth.

The reason one's self cannot achieve Truth no matter how much he desires it is falseness cannot achieve Truth however much it tries. Even if falseness does achieve Truth, it is still false.

If one is thankful to the method that allows him to completely discard his self and if he actually does throw away his false self and false world, he can be born in the land of Truth and become Truth.

Until now, we have only added to our minds while living in the world. It has always been this way, since we were young: in school and then in society, within the system and with its preconceptions we lived adding more and more to our minds. In the future, as we keep discarding and discarding again our false minds and bodies we will be reborn as the existence of God who is Truth. When this happens, man will be able to live righteously.

Maum Meditation is about discarding one's mind world and self. When one's mind world and self does not exist, only the Universe remains. Man will be complete when he is resurrected as the body and mind of the Universe, which is Truth and complete.

People have many sins and karma. Casting off all of one's karma and sins is the Maum Meditation method; it *is* Maum Meditation.

Those whose false selves try to achieve Truth will fail while those who recognize that their selves are ultimately useless and cast it off will be able to achieve Truth. The Bible tells us to deny our selves and follow Christ. It tells us that those who try to die will live whereas those who try to live will die. The Buddhist scriptures also tells us the way to completion is death and that the true world exists only when you die without anything remaining. Both of these scriptures are telling us that when one discards his false self, he will be reborn as Truth.

Those who were unable to complete this meditation could not achieve Truth because they tried to achieve it with their false selves.

What Is Salvation? It Is Falseness Becoming Truth

In Christianity it is said Christ, the Savior, will come down on a cloud with trumpeting angels. In Buddhism, it is said that *Maitreya* will come to the world of sentient beings, the *saha* world, to save people. *Jung-san* told us the Great Commander, *Dae-doo-mok*, will come, and *So-tae-san* also said that *Maitreya* will come.

The terms used above are all different but they denote the same existence.

They all refer to the empty space, the world's original master, coming as a human-being.

The master of the world is the master that made all of creation. The master is the existence of Truth. It is natural that this existence - the existence of *Jung* and *Shin* that is the source of this Universe - must come to the world in order for the world to be resurrected as the existence of *Jung* and *Shin*.

This existence is the place before all of creation came forth and because all of creation came forth from this place, this existence is the living Truth that is the Creator and true existence.

Countless people have tried to become Truth and failed. The reason they were unsuccessful despite their efforts is they were not Truth and a method to become Truth did not exist. Therefore, they could not know Truth.

If someone had achieved Truth, there would have been a method by which he had done so. People believe there have been many saints and enlightened people in the world, but if these people had truly been enlightened, a method would exist.

We seek and search in religion as well as other places in order to become complete because we are incomplete.

The existence spoken of in all religions is Truth. Man's salvation is becoming this existence - it is when man who is false becomes Truth.

The Way Forward For Mankind

In each country, people live making and being governed by the laws of the country in which they reside.

In Communist countries, it is people that govern, while in capitalist countries money governs over people. In any case, the laws that were made in order to make our lives comfortable have imprisoned us inside ourselves: they have had the adverse effect of trapping people within the law.

That is why those with money and power live good lives while those who are poor and weak struggle and live with hardship.

Mankind will be able to live as one when man discards his self and his mind world that are his conceptions and habits. Then, God's consciousness that is true - the world of *Jung* and *Shin* - will emerge. "My" conceptions and habits are my perspective only; if man lives with the big consciousness of God then he will live for others, concerned with the needs of other people. If man did not live only for himself, there would be no need for the law and the world would become righteous.

The way for us to live joyfully and without conflict is for everyone in the human race to each break down his own illusionary mind world and be resurrected in the world of Truth.

When man has something in his mind, it becomes suffering. When man lives with the true freedom of not possessing, the world will become one of never-ending laughter - it will become one.

When there is no conflict,
when there is no longer any *you* and *me*;
when we mutually help each other
so that others rather than one's self can succeed;
when it's no longer *my country* and *your country*
and we all become one;
there will be true value in human life.
The way forward for mankind is for all to repent.

Repentance is making man's mind, which is contrary to the mind of the world, become one with the world. In other words, being made to be reborn with the body and mind of God is repentance. When man becomes one with the world, all religions, ideologies, philosophies and learning will come from Truth, which is one. All people will unite and become Truth, and it will become a world of oneness.

What Is The End Of The World?

It is a common misconception that when the end of the world comes, the world will disappear.

It is said that when the end of the world comes, countless people will die while those who have faith in their religion will not.

Although many people predicted the time when the world will end, no one got it right because they did not know the true meaning of the end of the world. The end of the world - when all people die except for the faithful who are taken to heaven - will never come.

This misunderstanding has come about because the Bible, the Buddhist scriptures and other religious scriptures have been wrongly interpreted. A certain religion believed that their followers would physically levitate into the air and be taken to heaven. They waited for this event with over five hundred media representatives watching but the levitation never happened.

The true meaning of the end of the world is the end of man living in the false world - it is man being reborn as Truth in the true world. Levitation means man's consciousness, which had been confined in his mind world, is reborn as the true mind, the consciousness, of the great Universe itself. This is the true meaning of levitation into heaven.

The Buddhist scriptures, the Bible and other scriptures are Truth but they were all written figuratively. The reason each religion has been split into so many different sects is people are unable to interpret them with the mind of Truth and instead interpret them with their own conceptions and habits.

The end of the world is the time when falseness becomes Truth and it is also the time of salvation.

Unless falseness becomes Truth, the world and one's false self will disappear. This is the end of the world that people speak of - this is death.

Falseness is the world and all the other innumerable things man keeps inside his mind - it is the picture world.

We must be reborn in the true world after the picture world disappears. No one knows the true world or the false world, which is why people do not know the true meaning of the end of the world and live in fear.

People are so foolish - foolish enough to believe that only what is theirs and their own false ways of thinking are right.

Those who are consumed by their own religion or philosophies must find what is truly right by learning to accept other things.

If one is not Truth now, isn't he false? It is illogical for someone who is false to say he is right.

To put it differently, one must become Truth, interpret the true scriptures truly, know its true meaning, and he must become the true Truth.

Isn't this the way to live at the time of the end of the world?

We must keep our eyes wide open to whether a method to become Truth exists in the world. We must not meet the unlucky fate of our world coming to an end.

True Wisdom

We commonly speak of people having or not having wisdom.

Among the legends of King Solomon, there are stories illustrating his "wisdom". One story tells us how he distinguished real flowers from artificial flowers by opening a window and using a bee to show him which were real. Another story describes how he wisely helped to settle a quarrel between two women, each claiming to be the birth mother of a new-born baby.

However, man does not have any true wisdom because he lives inside his self-made false mind world of his conceptions and habits.

True wisdom is knowing the true principles of the world.

God is said to be omnipotent and omniscient. He is omnipotent because all creations were created by God and he is omniscient because he is the principles of the Universe itself. Man can only speak of his conceptions and habits that he has seen, heard and learned, but none of these things are at all correct from the point of view of God and the great Universe.

Everything from the viewpoint of one's self is falseness not wisdom, but from the viewpoint of God, the entire Universe, everything is

Truth.

When man's consciousness changes from one that is individual to that of the great Universe, he will be able to know all the ways of the world.

Where does man come from?

Why does he live, and where does he go after death?

When these questions are answered from one's own perspective, it cannot possibly be correct.

Man can only answer them from his own religious perspective, from the pictures he has taken and the books he has read. But the Universe that is God and the world, can know the answers all too clearly.

The place man came from is the world; the reason and purpose he lives is to become complete and live eternally; and when he dies if he lives inside his mind, he will live in hell that is an illusion, while he will live in the world if he has been born in the true world.

What then must man's state be in order to live forever?

The answer may seem easy when it is just heard, but it is not an easy question for man to actually answer. From the perspective of the true world, that is, when one has become the consciousness of the world, man will live forever if he is Truth and he will die if he is false. This is why we have religion and other spiritual organizations.

But if one has not become Truth, then isn't he completely false?

How can man become complete? From the world's point of view, he will become Truth when he eliminates his false world and false self.

There can only be true wisdom when one's individual consciousness is resurrected into the consciousness of God. Only a person who has been resurrected as God will know the ways of the world and have the wisdom to know righteousness.

Man Does Not Know Anything And All Of His Words And Actions Are False

Our minds are formed from a young age, through our daily lives: from our experiences with our families, neighborhood, schools and society. As our minds form, we come to have standards for what we like and dislike, and what we think of as right and wrong and good and bad.

Man, by nature, takes pictures of the whole world within him and stores these past pictures of memories as photos; he is false because the pictures are what speak and move.

What man knows is false because it is the pictures that see and speak. Therefore, he does not actually know anything.

There is true knowing when man becomes Truth and is no longer false - when he becomes living God. Only then does he truly *know.*

Completion is the state where all knowledge cease to exist, but at the same time it is also the state of wisdom itself. Thus, it can know everything. But for a man, whose existence is false, it is falseness that speaks and lives which is why it is said that man knows nothing.

For example, the knowledge that comes from having memorized a religious scripture like the Bible or the Buddhist sutras is false because it comes from the pictures that one has taken of that scripture. No matter how saintly one pretends to be or how intelligently one speaks, his words and actions are false if there is no Truth within him.

Man lives, speaks and acts according to the pictures he has, pictures that have no true knowledge. This is the reason man is false.

The words and actions of a person who has become Truth are true.

Nothing Is Right In Man's World

People are born without knowing the reason or purpose of their birth and then die ignorant of what everyone should fundamentally know: the value of life, where one goes after he dies, whether it is possible to live forever, whether or not heaven actually exists, and the ways of the world.

Suppose you are a dog or a bird, or some other animal. You would only be able to think like those animals and unable to understand the will of people. Similarly, man does not know he is living inside a picture, a false picture world, because he lives inside the false world that he has made from the pictures he has taken from birth. He believes that the stored illusionary pictures are himself, which lead him to live a self-centered life, thinking that he is right and everyone else is wrong.

All creations were made through the balance and harmony of heaven and earth, and heaven and earth are originally complete. However there is nothing right about man or man's world because he has turned away from heaven and earth, and lives copying them.

Think about the life that you led today: didn't you take pictures in your mind the whole day and weren't you within those pictures? During that time, the true world did not exist.

A person who lives in the real world, and not in the world of pictures, lives with the mind of the world; such a person is complete and does not take pictures.

Let's suppose you worked the whole day: for an ordinary person, the work he did exists in his mind but it does not exist in the mind of a person born in the true world, even though he works in the same way. This is because he does not have a world of pictures.

If we do not live in the world by becoming one with the world's *Jung* and *Shin*, the evil and sinful world we live in without meaning or purpose - the world where we have turned against the world of God and where we have taken pictures of the world of God inside us - has nothing right within it.

Sins Committed In The Mind Are Sins

The Bible states that sins committed in our minds are also sins.

God's mind is one of goodness, kindness and virtue, while the human mind is an evil mind of sin.

Since the human mind is a possessive mind, it copies the world and all that happens in the world to make its own individual mind. Inside this self-made mind, man forms his conceptions and habits - this is sin.

In other words, thinking something is right when it is consistent with one's perspective while considering it to be wrong when it is not, judging something to be bad or good - such minds are delusions, and delusions beget more delusions which form one's self. This is what sin is.

Even twins born on the same day at the same time have different minds. Therefore naturally parents, siblings, spouses and children all have different minds from each other. This is the reason behind all conflicts. Even in politics, conflicts happen because of different mindsets.

When the possessive human mind is discarded, God remains.

The mind of God is the place beyond sin. There are no sins in God's mind because human preconceptions and habits do not exist there.

Sins exist in the human mind because it is the mind of possession. The mind of God is absent of the mind of possession, and therefore it has not possessed any minds. This is why God's mind is free of sin.

In the Buddhist scriptures, there is a saying that everything is made in the mind. This means man's delusions produce tens of thousands of different minds, while God's mind creates everything in heaven and earth by the balance and harmony of heaven and earth.

Man Is A Ghost

We are afraid of ghosts and we also often tell stories about ghosts. A ghost is an illusion that believes it exists.

Man does not live in the world but in his mind world - an illusionary world. Isn't man who lives in an illusionary world also an illusion?

Man believes it is his illusionary self that lives, that it is this entity that dies, that it is this self that is right or wrong, sinful or not sinful. However all of these things are within his illusionary mind. Therefore, these things are ghosts because they are not real.

The human mind changes night and day, and there are many occasions when a promise made in the morning is broken by evening.

The human mind is an illusion because man lives as a picture in a self-centered picture world. Christ said that a righteous person does not exist among men. A righteous person is someone who is right and true but a righteous person does not exist because all men are false and not Truth.

In the world, there is not one righteous person; not even amongst our parents, siblings, spouses, children, between couples or friends. There is no one who can be trusted.

Everyone lives a self-centered life - they live for their own benefit, in their own conceptions. When people who are illusions and ghosts are resurrected as true people, as God, they will become true, and they will be able to believe in each other and live as one.

Man is a ghost because he is an illusion, an entity that does not exist in the true world.

For The World To Become Complete

In Buddhism, it is said that someday this world will become paradise and in Christianity, they pray for God's will to be done on earth as it is in heaven. These words refer to the world becoming one and complete - a world of complete Truth. The world however, is already complete.

Only man is dead within his mind world so when man is saved, this world becomes paradise; when man is saved the will of God will have been done in this world just as it is in heaven. In other words, the world will become complete and true. For this to happen, man must escape from his mind world which is non-existent and false, and come out into the world that is true. The mind world is a tomb, made by pictures. It is hell and a world of death. Only when one is reborn from the mind world into the true world can the world become complete.

Completion is when everything has been fulfilled and there is an eternity without death. Even though this world *is* the complete world, man does not live in the world. Therefore he will be reborn when his false self and mind world no longer exists.

Do You Know Where You Will Go After You Die?

People live without knowing the reason they were born and then they die and pass on to the next world. Since the beginning of time countless people have lived and died. The correct answer to the title above can only be known after one dies and goes to the next world. No one has ever known the answer because no one has ever truly died.

In the Bible and Buddhist scriptures, it is said that "good" people will go to heaven and that "bad" people will go to hell. Everyone who is born in the world must eventually die, but those who are fearful of death are comforted by their religion. However only a few people, or perhaps none, are certain of where they go after they die. Many have put in a great effort to find the answer, but there is no one who actually knows.

While man is living in the world, he lives from the energy drawn from the food he eats. What happens when his body disappears? Man does not have the answer to this question. Only the sky - Truth, the great Universe, the Creator - knows the answer.

Let's think about things from the perspective of the sky, the great Universe. Where did and where will the many people who lived or are now living in the world go? Those who live inside their mind worlds - which are illusions and pictures that overlap the real world - will go to their mind worlds because it is all they have. Those who have become one with the world will be reborn and live in the world. It is the mind that sees, hears, speaks and smells. Therefore, even when the body passes away, one who is reborn in the true world will live forever because he is Truth and without death.

From the viewpoint of the sky, the Universe, the world of illusion copied from the real world does not exist - therefore a person who lives within this world also does not exist.

Hell exists, but does not exist; does not exist and yet exists. Hell does not exist. The self-made non-existent world that one traps himself into of his own accord is hell. Just as everyone lives according to what they have in their minds, a person who has this illusionary world in his mind mistakenly believes that he is alive. Everyone who dies, without exception, goes to hell that is death itself. Only those who have been resurrected as Truth while they are living will live forever in the land of Truth. We must go to heaven and attain eternal life while we are still alive.

People commonly believe that they will go to heaven or hell after they die. No one knows what heaven is, because they are already living in hell. Only a person who has been born in heaven knows both heaven and hell. Only when one's self disappears from the world is it possible to be resurrected in the complete world of God. There is a Korean saying that you can know the afterworld only after you die.

Man can only know the afterworld if he has completely died while he is still living and only such a person will be reborn as Truth and live forever. One must die in order to be reborn or resurrected, for how can it happen otherwise?

When one who has a "self" physically dies, he will go to hell that is true death. All people will go to hell because no one has died while living. No one in this world has died and no one has been resurrected, and because they are not Truth, they will all go to hell.

What Is Samsara (The Eternal Cycle Of Birth, Death And Rebirth)?

Many people have questions about *samsara*. The world was created by the Creator and because the Creator is Truth and complete, the world is also complete. However, man is not complete so he seeks to become so through religion or other practices.

Samsara exists because the incomplete human mind world contains tens of thousands of incomplete minds. When man dies, he roams around and around his mind world - an illusionary world of pictures. This is *samsara*. *Samsara* is wandering trapped inside the world one has made with the innumerable minds he has. From the viewpoint of Truth, this illusion does not exist, and man also does not exist because he lives within the illusion.

The way to escape from *samsara* is to destroy one's mind world that is an illusion and hell and be reborn in the true world. He who is born in the true world has no *samsara* - he is an eternal, never-dying, divine entity and will live forever with freedom and liberation.

The False Mind, The Original Mind

Man has continually added or "eaten" minds by storing countless different events and pictures of the world in his mind. In other words, he has only ever added to his mind.

Completion is when pictures of the Universe and the picture world do not exist at all and one is reborn as *Jung* and *Shin*. In such a state, one is able to just exist, just live, without delusions or worries. It is a place where all knowledge has ceased and there is nothing further to know or be curious about. No judgment or discrimination exist because one is always the mind of the Universe - the divine mind. One is wisdom itself because he is the divine consciousness that is alive. Because he is liberated from everything even though he is alive, he is the mind of oneness itself.

How Can One Know Truth?

Christians are waiting for the new Messiah to come and Buddhists are waiting for *Maitreya*. They are waiting for the Savior of the world but the existence of their conceptions that they are waiting for will never come no matter how long they wait. The true Savior is an existence of complete Truth, an existence who is true and real. This existence will not come in the shape and form of Jesus Christ or Buddha from thousands of years ago, but he is nevertheless the Savior because he will make people become Truth.

The reason man cannot know Truth is he lives within his own mind world and does not have Truth in him, therefore even if Truth comes he will be unable to recognize him. Only those who are alive - those who have become Truth - will be able to recognize Truth. The Bible says that people will not know when Truth, Christ, comes. This is because people are false and do not have Truth within them.

Man often tries to find Truth within his conceptions and habits but man cannot know Truth because Truth does not exist within human conceptions.

Only those who have become Truth can know Truth. He who is

alive can recognize who is alive and who is dead. Only those who are true can know both Truth and falseness. Thus, only he who has become true can know what is true and only he who has been born in the true world can know the ways of the world. Man thinks he is living in the world but he is actually living inside his mind and not the world. Therefore he must be born in the world in order to know the ways of heaven and earth.

Do Heaven And Hell Truly Exist?

Many people are curious about heaven and hell - about where they are and whether or not they truly exist.

What happens when man dies? Everyone has thought about it at least once, but there are no clear answers. People have vague ideas that they will go to heaven if they have faith in their religion, if they get rid of their karma and sins, or if they do good deeds.

Man lives in hell - a non-existent picture world - from the moment he is born. Through his eyes, nose, ears, mouth and body he copies into his mind world everything in the world - all that he has seen, heard, smelled, spoken and sensed with his body as well as everything he has experienced. He puts the world and all that belongs to the world in his mind, and he believes that he is living in the real world because his mind world overlaps the real world. In the same way a video is produced, the human mind duplicates the world and everything that belongs to the world into his mind and lives within it. This is the reason man is a sinner; why he lives with karma.

When one dies after living in this world of false images, he goes to this picture world. This is hell. It is said in Buddhism that when a person dies, he will follow his karma and karmic ties. This means that he goes to the illusionary world that he himself has made; he ends up dying because this world is false and not true. This is what hell is.

The dreams that we dream at night do not exist, but yet they do. Likewise, hell also does not exist from the standpoint of the real world but it exists in the way dreams do. One must eliminate this hell - his mind world and his self - for then, it is heaven.

The world God created is already complete and it is already enlightened. What this means is the world is completion itself and is thus, everlastingly alive. But man is trapped within his own mind of karma and sin and he is not born in the world. Therefore, the way for man to go to heaven is to get rid of his sins and karma while he is living and be reborn in the world of heaven where there is no death. Hell is one's mind world, the illusionary picture world, and it is a world that does not exist in the real world. Heaven is this world, which is Truth.

Going To The Complete World While Living

The Bible compares entering the kingdom of heaven to a camel passing through the eye of a needle. This means it is practically impossible for man to go to heaven. It also says that the poor in spirit are blessed for theirs will be the kingdom of heaven. To be poor in spirit is to have nothing in one's mind - to have "no minds". If one does not have any minds, the place he is in is the kingdom of God, Christ and Truth. This is why religions ask us to cleanse and empty our minds. What we are told in Christianity and in other religions all have the same message.

In order to go to heaven, one must have no human minds. Man's mind is one that has turned against the world of God. He lives in the world of his own video which was made by copying the world that belongs to God - this is man's sin and karma. This is what makes man a sinner, and the reason he has karma.

If one eliminates the video that is sin and an illusion, as well as one's self, the world that is real will emerge and he will become one with the world. When man is reborn in the world of Truth while living, he is born in heaven. Doesn't it go against reason that one who has not become Truth while living can go to the real living world that is heaven after he is dead? It is only natural that what is false dies and disappears. Only what is real can live in the real world.

The True Meaning Behind "The Faithful Will Go To Heaven"

Christianity tells us we must believe in Christ if we are to go to heaven and that faith in Christ is the only thing needed to go to heaven. This is certainly very true. Believing in Truth is the prerequisite condition to enter heaven, and only Christ is Truth so we must believe in Truth to get there.

You can only have faith if you become one. Christ is Truth - therefore when you believe in Christ and follow him, you will be able to go to the land of Truth and Christ. Without believing in Truth, you cannot go to heaven. One must believe in Truth and become Truth in order to go to heaven. In other words, one must believe in what is real and become real in order to go to the real world.

What Is Real (Truth), What is Fake (Falseness)

There is not one person who is living in the real world. The sky of the infinite great Universe is the origin, the source, and the Creator. This Creator consists of a great Soul and Spirit. In other words, it has a body and mind. This existence is Truth itself that existed before the beginning and will exist after the world ends. It is the mother and father of all creation and it is the Creator that created all things.

This existence is complete and all things born in the world are the children of this existence. They were created as complete entities and they were made to live but man has turned against the Creator. He copies the world of the Creator and what belongs to the Creator and he has a copied world in his mind. Only man has a mind world and only man is fake. If man were complete, he would not need religion or other similar organizations.

What is real is the world. The world is already complete and the world is already enlightened. When our minds are reborn as the body and mind of the great Universe itself that is alive, we will not die because this existence is God. Furthermore we will know all the ways of the world because this existence is wisdom.

What is false is man and Truth is the world. Man should not live in his own mind world, the illusionary world; he should be born in the true world.

One Can Go To Heaven Only When He Has Completely Eliminated His Sins And Karma

Man was born with a mind that takes pictures of the world and everything that belongs to the world. All of our parents and ancestors died after living in illusions, in pictures taken of the world. This is the reason our minds by nature and from birth are like a film of pictures. We live speaking and acting according to what is scripted in this film. But just as a picture is not real, the film is false. Man's mind itself is sin and karma. Without discarding the picture world and one's self that is a picture, man cannot be born into the world that is heaven.

Doesn't the true world exist when one's individual mind world and one's self no longer exist? One can be resurrected in the true world when one's self and mind world no longer exist. The true world will emerge when one's self and mind world have been completely eliminated. When a person is one with the consciousness of heaven in every moment and regardless of where he is, he will be born in heaven. One must be completely born, a hundred percent, as the Soul and Spirit, the Energy and God, of Truth that is heaven. Only when one is born in heaven while living can he go to heaven.

Only Truth Can Make One Become Truth

The original existence of Truth in the world is the empty sky - the place that existed before all creations of heaven and earth came forth. This existence is the original Truth, and the creations of heaven and earth that came forth from this place are also Truth. The existence of Truth, the origin, is not material but a Soul and Spirit. This metaphysical real existence is omnipotent and omniscient so it was able to create the world.

Each religion speaks of a Savior - a Messiah or *Maitreya* who will come to the world. It is when this existence of Truth comes in human form that man will also be able to become Truth. Just as beans are needed in order to produce more beans, and there must be rice in order to produce more rice, Truth must exist in order for Truth to appear. When the existence of Truth comes to the world, it is possible for man to become Truth. The reason man does not know what falseness or Truth are, is he lives within falseness and his consciousness is dead. Only when the existence of Truth exists is it possible for more existences of Truth to appear; only then is it possible for man who is false to become Truth.

Maum Meditation is a place where falseness can be made into Truth. It is where one discards all of his false self and becomes reborn as the real body and mind of the Universe. Salvation is also falseness becoming Truth. Rebirth and resurrection can only be done by a person of the true world. Only a person of the true world can take one to the true world. This is because there is no Truth in the human world.

What Is Wisdom?

In the false human world, crafty people are often said to have wisdom. However, such tricks and stratagems are not wisdom but merely ways of life in the human world. Man's words and actions all take place within the picture world, the mind world that he has made, so all of his words and actions are not real but false. No matter how like a saint a person may speak or behave, his words and actions are false and fake because they were spoken and done by a picture.

Wisdom is knowing the ways of Truth. Regardless of how articulately one speaks or how well he preaches, if he does so inside an illusion it is not true, but false. Only the Creator that is Truth has wisdom. Man can also become wisdom itself if his human body and mind are reborn as the true body and mind of the Universe. One must change his individual conceptions and habits and see from the perspective of the Universe in order to see truly.

True wisdom is knowing the ways of the world once one has become the viewpoint of the Universe that is God, or in other words, once one has become the consciousness of the Universe. The Bible, the Buddhist sutras and other scriptures are Truth and were all written from the consciousness of the Universe. Man is not able to interpret them correctly nor is he able to know their true meaning because Truth does not exist within man. Only the consciousness of the Universe, which is God and the whole, has wisdom and knows all the ways of the world.

One person asked me why he did not have any wisdom. I told him it is because he had not entered the place of Truth and he has not been born from the place of Truth. While man may wish for wisdom in his own mind world, it is only when his self that seeks wisdom is completely dead and gone that true wisdom will appear.

Truth Remains Once All Falseness Have Been Destroyed

There is a Korean saying that goes, "*Huh, huh, cham*, I'm at a loss for words!"

Huh, huh, cham (an interjection or exclamatory remark that literally means "false, false, Truth") means once all falseness have been eliminated, Truth will emerge. While living in this world, the world of illusion, we have only learned how to add to our minds.

In other words, as we lived seeing, hearing, speaking, smelling, we only acquired more minds of greed - the mind that wants to possess all sorts of things, and the entire world. The sum of these minds has become our present selves.

There is no end to the mind that wants to have more. The more one has, the more false pictures he gets, which turn into burden and suffering. When we get rid and get rid again of all falseness, in the end only Truth will remain. Falseness eventually disappears when you eliminate it because it is false, but Truth always remains as it is, no matter how hard you try to destroy it because it is true.

Truth is what remains at the very end.

He who has erased all falseness is a true person.

Why Man Needs To Be Saved

If man were complete and true, then religion and other places where people strive to become Truth would not exist and man would not be waiting for the Messiah or *Maitreya*.

It is said in the Bible that human sin has existed since Adam and Eve ate the fruit of good and evil. In actuality, a fruit of good and evil did not really exist - it is just a figurative way of saying that man sowed the concept of good and evil into his mind. That man "ate" such mind, such fruit, means that he put conceptions of what good and evil are into his mind - this is what sin is. The individual betrayed the whole that is the great Creator and "ate" all kinds of things that belong to the world. Therefore man lives in sin and is dead within that sin.

During the period of the Universe when man was incomplete, the human population increased rapidly. During this time, the greed of the human race drove the rapid development of civilization. People often ask why God did not make man complete if he himself is complete. It must have been the unintended intention of the sky to make human life incomplete so that the human population would increase and as many people as possible in the world can be saved. If the human race had been created complete from the beginning it may have already become extinct.

The sky, heaven, is silent but the world moves according to its will. Heaven must one day come as a human-being in order for salvation to happen. To save man, that is, if man is to escape from the world of sin and be born in the world of Truth, a person of the true world must come. Man thinks he lives according to his own human will, but although the Universe that is the Creator does not have any intentions or plans, it will, without fail, come as a true person from the world of Truth to save people.

This is the unintended intention, the will, of the Universe. Once the population has reached its peak according to the will of the Universe, it will save many people.

Man's salvation is falseness becoming Truth.

Only the existence of Truth can save man by making him become Truth. Man needs to be saved because he is false; he needs to be made into Truth. This is the role of Truth.

Part 2

The age of incompletion was one of man ever-adding to his mind, but the age of completion is a time of subtracting the human mind.

Dō Is The Ordinary

Dō literally means "path".

To do *dō* or to seek Truth means to walk a path, the destination being to get to Truth. When Jesus said, "I am the Way, the Truth and the Life", the "I" in the sentence refers to Truth. Going to Truth is the way, truth and life.

The world is complete and Truth - the shapes and forms of everything created and where they were placed is Truth and completion. The world just as it is made is *dō.*

People do *dō* because they want to become extraordinary. They want to have abilities such as being able to cure illness, or fly, or be superior to ordinary people in some way.

But illness is cured in hospitals by doctors and medicine, and people cannot fly because they do not have wings. *Dō* is people living in the world according to nature's flow, without behaving in a delusional way. That is, *dō* is people simply living, eating and walking as people do.

It has become habitual for people to live constantly wanting to gain something but this only brings suffering and burden. A person who tries to possess or gain something will become possessed by that mind to the extent of how much of this mind he has in him. Such a person will not be able to achieve *dō*.

In order for falseness to become Truth, it must be eliminated. If a false ghost tries to achieve Truth without dying, it remains a ghost. *Dō* is completely discarding the ghost that is false and being reborn as Truth. A person who has been born as Truth is the most ordinary: he does not know anything extraordinary and he does not speak either of extraordinary things or the ghost world. He will simply just live.

To just live is to be the mind of the Universe itself: to sleep when it is time to sleep, and to eat when it is time to eat. A person who has this mind does not have any false minds. There is only Truth within him so all of his actions are true. All things done when one has the mind of the Universe are true - all things done by a person who has become one with the mind of the Universe are true.

Dō is the ordinary. It is the world. It is to live as one with the world. The world is just as you see it, it is just the way it exists.

The World Is As You See It, Just As It Exists

Many people believe there are people in the world with rare abilities such as flying, walking on water, travelling over long distances within a short space of time, or some other supernatural ability. People are full of delusions - some people believe someone will come to the world on a cloud, or that a dead person will come back to the world from heaven. Only man lives with these kinds of delusional thoughts because he has delusions in his mind.

Truth is the world just as you see it, just as it exists. Man cannot fly because he does not have wings. He does not have any special powers and he cannot perform miracles. Everything lives and dies in the way that they have been placed in the world according to the universal order of nature. However a person who has been born with the Soul and Spirit of the Universe will live eternally in the world of the Universe that is true.

A true miracle is to make what is false become something real. Everything that is made and everything that exists, is made and exists through its karmic ties. What was formed without conditions or reason - to simply just be formed - will just live according to its form and shape, the way it was formed. It will live according to its surrounding conditions.

Dō is not about gaining something that benefits oneself or about gaining special abilities. It is about eliminating one's self, and getting to know the Universe as it is. It is about knowing that the Universe is alive. Only he who has been born into Truth will not try to gain abilities or perform miracles. He will not pretend to know about supernatural things, which are in any case incorrect.

From Negativity To Positivity

The human mind is a negative mind. It is a self-centered mind. It only knows and cares about itself so it is negative about anything that is outside of what it knows. Only things that exist within it are regarded as being correct; anything it does not know or have are thought to be wrong. The human mind is negative - it insists that only it is right and is not able to acknowledge and accept all things.

You cannot possibly succeed at a task if you believe that it cannot be done. However, if you have a positive mind-set and believe that it can be done, you will succeed. Even in the human world, a negative person cannot be successful. Such a person is where he is because he is small-minded. On the other hand, a positive person has a "big" mind - he is broad-minded.

If you are able to accept everything that is said about you, even when you are spoken of in a negative way, none of what is said will remain in your mind. However if you are unable to accept what is said and begin to think of the person who said them as your enemy, those words will remain in your mind. You will then have to carry the mind of non-acceptance eternally.

A person with a positive mind is one who does not possess his own individual mind. He is someone who has become the mind of the Universe. Everyone in the world believes that they are great - they are unable to accept and acknowledge others because they do not have the positive mind of God, the mind of the Universe.

From the world's point of view, the other countless things living in this true world are all living in their own way. They just live, and are able to accept everything without being concerned with this or that. The true world just lives without being biased towards any one side.

All people would have positive minds if they lived with the mind of the world that just exists. It would be the end of all conflict, and days of never-ending laughter would follow because the world's mind is the mind of oneness. Everyone will live well when all people change their negative minds to positive minds.

From Non-existence To Existence

The reason and purpose the world was created was so the world and everything in it could be reborn with the body and mind of the Universe and Creator - as eternally living, never-dying immortals. However, man does not know the will of the origin - the meaning behind the creation of the world - because he is dead and trapped inside his mind.

Man is an entity that does not exist in the world. He is dead, trapped inside his mind. If he becomes one with the world and sees from the world's point of view, this world is the complete land of God and everything that exists is also God.

Suppose that there are no people in the world. A world without people has no meaning or purpose. Without people, it does not matter whether or not the world exists. The best way forward for man is to be reborn in the world. Being born in the world, and only this, is salvation and human completion.

Man mistakenly believes that he is living in the world, but it is precisely because he does not live in the world that he needs to be born in the world by cleansing his mind. This is what it is to be born into existence from non-existence.

What meaning is there in being born in the world only to live for seventy-odd years? The only salvation is being born into existence from non-existence. One's life, what one learns in the world, and all that happens in the world of a ghost, are illusions. Therefore one can become an eternal and never-dying immortal only when he comes out into the world, and becomes one with the original Creator in the real, true world. Then, he will become one with the original world and live according to the ways of the world - according to nature's flow. He will always be joyful for he will be in the world of joy. He will be filled with gratitude for he will be alive after being non-existent. He will be thankful for being alive, as well as for all things.

The original Creator does not have form and shape, but all things that exist are the Creator and the children of the Creator. The Creator which created all things, created the world into existence from non-existence - from conditions that are the "cause" to existence that is the "result" - by the harmony and balance of nature which is nature's flow. Likewise, man will also live according to nature's flow.

Man must be saved for both man and the world to live.

What Exists In the World Exists, And What Does Not Exist In The World Does Not Exist

There are many, many things in the world. In the past when there were no elephants, giraffes or monkeys in Korea, some people did not believe they existed.

It was foretold in a book of prophecy that people in the future would have wisdom and be able to see places thousands of leagues away from where they are sitting. Today we are able to see things thousands of miles away all around the world via television. The origin of the world, the Creator, created all creations according to universal order. People have also helped plant and animal populations to multiply.

There are stories in each religion about people going to heaven. There are also similar stories in Korean folk legends, such as the story of the snail-wife, the children who became a star and moon, the thousand year-old fox girl, as well as many others.

These stories are sometimes taken literally but these are misinterpretations. A person who is born in the true world that is righteous can interpret them correctly but those who are trapped inside the human mind cannot interpret these stories, or the stories in the Bible and Buddhist scriptures. All scriptures were written from the perspective of the world and not from the individual human perspective. When man becomes one with the world, it is possible to know the ways of the world, what is true and false, as well as all of Truth.

The world is just as one sees it, it is just as it exists, but those who have a false world cannot see it just as it is and as it exists. They can only speak and act according to what they have in their illusionary worlds. Only that which exists in the world actually exists, and what does not exist in the world - that which only exists in man's mind - does not exist. The world can be seen correctly only when man becomes one with the mind of the world.

To Be Reborn Or Resurrected, One Must First Die

I have often heard religious people say they have been resurrected as the Holy Spirit and then later change their minds. One can only be resurrected or reborn after he has completely discarded his body and mind, which are his sins and karma.

People who speak as if they can foresee or know things, have not truly been resurrected. They are the most pitiful people in the world and they are dead because they are ghosts within their own mind world, the picture world. They are those who have been born inside an illusion, their own delusional world, while they are living. They live as slaves of this falseness and their souls die and disappear forever in a world that does not exist in the real world.

One can be reborn and resurrected only when one completely eliminates his self and his entire illusionary world that he has made.

Man's Sin

Man's sin is dwelling in an illusion. He who is within human conceptions and habits has sins but he who is free from everything does not have any sins. The place free from sins and karma is the place of *dō.* It is a place of Truth that is free from everything in the human world. The place of Truth is a place where one has discarded all of his conceptions and habits, the place where even one's self does not exist. It is a place free from absolutely everything - a place of freedom, deliverance and liberation.

The real metaphysical entity of the Creator is the Soul and Spirit of the Universe - the origin. The place before all creations of heaven and earth were created is the Universe's Soul and Spirit that is without form. Although this place has no form, it is an existence that is alive. Everything in heaven and earth came from this place and return to it. This existence is the Universe itself, it exists of and by itself and it is an existence that just exists. Although this existence does not have shape or form, it is alive and it is the source and the Creator of all things in heaven and earth. Just as you can only know what New York is like when you have been to New York, only those who have become this existence itself can know this existence.

The place where there is absolutely nothing is the Universe's body and amidst the nothingness, the one God exists. This existence is the Soul and Spirit of the Universe. This Soul and Spirit where there is nothing is called Buddha, God and Allah in each respective religion. The Soul and Spirit is called *Dharmakaya* and *Sambhogakaya*; it is also called the Holy Spirit and Holy Father and this place is the source and Creator of all things. All of heaven and earth's creation came from this place, and are representations of this place. Everything is born from certain conditions and lives according to certain conditions. This is the law of cause and effect. It is the law of nature that when there is a cause a result follows.

The world and everything that happened in the world had been taken as pictures in my mind. I had lived in an illusion, a picture. I mistakenly believed that I lived in the world because my mind had overlapped the world.

Those Who Have Sold Out Their True Souls

Man does not know what Truth is. That is, he does not know what is true and righteous. His conceptions are formed from what he has seen, heard, learned and experienced and he believes that only what agrees with his conceptions are correct. However all things are just a difference in perspective and in man's life nothing is actually correct. This is because in man it is not Truth but falseness that speaks and moves. Pictures become stored in the "video" that is his mind, and it is the pictures that speak, hear and move.

What is correct or righteous, is Truth and the world that is true. A person who has become one with the world, or in other words, he who has been reborn with the mind of the world, is righteous - a person who has been born with the consciousness of the Universe. Such a person does not die because he is an existence that is eternal and never-dying. Those who are not born as Truth - those who do not achieve human completion - will end up dying forever.

The ordinary person lives in the ghost world of his mind, an illusionary world. There are also those who say they have come from heaven, that they are heavenly Gods, and speak as if they know things. These people will live eternally in the world of hell because their souls have been born in an illusion while they are living. They end up dying forever because the masters of their selves are delusional illusions. An illusion is like a dream and it does not exist. Because it is not real, it is death. Only that which is real lives.

People believe that *dō* is about being able to do supernatural acts or speaking as if one knows supernatural things, but real *dō* is not about speaking of ghostly things. One has "come from heaven" if he has become one with heaven. A person who saw an image of himself coming down from heaven in his delusions did not truly come from heaven. Such a person has come from his delusional mind world, which is an illusion. If man discards his self he will be reborn as the Universe's body and mind. However this process is difficult, and because man is foolish he has a tendency to fall back into the illusionary world. What is described above is the type of *dō* practiced by traitors who act against heaven. The things one knows with the consciousness of the Universe is wisdom itself, whereas the things one knows through the images inside himself are those of the lowest-level ghost. They are manifestations of one's greed because he has not been able to achieve *dō*.

All people who speak of knowing things from the illusions they see within their mind worlds need to sincerely repent because they are those who have sold out their true souls. They will end up dying and suffering in hell for eternity.

A Complete Person

Education began a long time ago. In the past, education in Korea focused on character-building. The emphasis was on memorizing the words of saints, and striving to act in a similar way. In recent times, education has changed to specializing in a certain field.

Education of the "whole person" or the "complete person" is commonly spoken of, but the definition of a complete person in education and the way to become so is unclear.

In China, a complete person is called *ji yin yong*. In Korea it is thought that a complete person must be wise, *ji*, virtuous, *deok*, and courageous, *che*, so the word has been changed to *ji deok che* and this term has been used in schools.

A true complete person is a person who is true; a whole and complete person is one who is real. Although there is a great emphasis on being educated and there are many educational institutions, there is no place that offers the education to truly become a complete person.

The world currently has divisions between nations, gaps between the wealthy and the poor, those who are superior and those who are inferior. There is a lack of trust between people and the world is a divided place that is unable to unite and become one.

More than anything, educators who are in the front lines of education need to become complete people and educating people to become complete should be the first priority. Only then can education be a proper one. Put in another way, the world will become brighter when man first becomes a true person before studying a specialization. If man lives for others, knowing the value of life and the reason he is born in the world, he will be able to live a joy-filled life.

Until now we have lived only for ourselves. We need to think at least once about what we have achieved by living in this way. If one wants to become an educator who can hold his head up high, he himself needs to become complete, and help his colleagues, family and students to become complete people.

Man can become true when he discards his human mind world and his false self that is living inside that mind. When he discards it all, only Truth remains and he will be reborn as a true, complete person.

To be complete is to be without death and anyone can become a saint if he is resurrected as Truth itself. Maum Meditation is the only institution that offers education of the whole person so I hope that educators will flock to this place and help to bring light to the world.

Only then can our world, the world of our descendents, become brighter; only then will it become one, where all can live a life of joy and all men will be able to live with true values, and know the value of life.

Woo Myung

What Man Needs To Achieve And Do

What is it that you are trying to gain,
trying to find,
trying to obtain,
and trying to have?

There has never been anything to gain, have or possess in human life because human life itself is a futile illusion. No one in the world is righteous because people live inside their minds. Everyone lives greedily, acquiring countless false and useless things, and they suffer within that falseness while always wanting to have more.

What then, must man achieve and do?

Man can become a true person and righteous one if he escapes from his burden and lives reborn in the world. Such a person lives without death. A person's level of affluence is decided by what kind of mind he has - by what kind of minds he has "eaten" - and not by his will. However these kinds of things are meaningless. Becoming Truth and living and working in the true world, and only this, is completion. This is what man needs to do and it is also the most "human" way to live.

Time just exists, silently, yet at the same time, it exists as a passing existence in man's life. In the world of the mind, there is no past, present or future. The Bible asks us to look at the birds flying in the sky and the flowers blooming in the fields. This means nature and the animals in nature have neither a past nor thoughts about the future so they are able to just live.

People live with worries because they think about the future with the mind of the past. But they need not worry, that is, those who are living in the land of Truth need not worry if they are able to survive in the present. They can live well without being anxious about the future. This is because heaven has fulfilled everything - it is enough to be able to eat and survive in the present and there is no need to worry about the future.

It is enough to work diligently right now - only a person who is inside a picture worries about how he will live in the future. Man is a false ghost because he lives inside an illusion, and a false ghost only cares about himself. He cares only for his own security - namely, he lives worrying about his body. However a person who has been born in the land of Truth will sacrifice his whole body to work in the land of Truth.

It is enough if you are able to eat and live now. Do not worry about the future and work diligently. Everything in great nature just lives. Man should follow its example by not worrying, and like nature, just live as a member of nature.

Chundo (Prayers Or Rites For The Passage Of The Dead Into Heaven)

Maum Meditation is the study and practice of the method to go to the land of Truth while one is still living. It is what Buddhism calls *ye su je* (Buddhist rites of passage to heaven for the living) which is to send oneself to the land of Truth. Maum Meditation is like performing *chundo* for one's self while he is still living.

Many religions, shamans, and other organizations also have similar rites to *chundo*. When such kinds of rites or prayers are performed, the dead end up going to the mind world of the person performing them. If the person performing them is Truth, the dead go to the land of Truth; if he is false, they go to a false world.

If you are not Truth right now, the place where you worship or practice is false. Moreover, if a place has not been able to make a living person become Truth, then the rites performed there are also false.

Maum Meditation makes living people become Truth, and *chundo* performed at Maum Meditation is able to send people to the land of Truth. It is able to do so because these things can only be done by Truth.

Many People Ask If Maum Meditation Is A Religion

Until now, people in religions listened to the words of saints, spoke about them, and strove to behave accordingly. Religions are places where people go to listen to the words of saints because they are incomplete. Religions are also places where one must believe those words and adhere to them. But more importantly, people have been unable to become complete in these places because they lack a concrete method.

Becoming complete is to become an eternally-living, never-dying immortal by becoming Truth. In other words, you are complete only when you become an existence that never dies. The existence of Truth is the Soul and Spirit of the great Universe. This existence existed an eternity before, it exists now, and it will exist and live an eternity after. It is the Creator. Everything created in the world is Truth. They are all enlightened and complete in the land of God and they exist without death. Only man is dead. His body and mind are living in an illusionary picture. For these reasons, the ultimate goal of Maum Meditation is to help man discard his illusionary body and mind and change to the body and mind of the Universe - the real, forever-living, never-dying, immortal.

This, and only this, is the method to become Truth, and only this is true. Religion is something that exists in one's mind. The true consciousness is beyond one's conceptions and habits - when a person does not have anything in his mind that is his, and he becomes one with the Universe that is God, it is possible for him to transcend religion and become a complete existence.

Maum Meditation is the place where you transcend religion and become resurrected as the child of God and Truth. Maum Meditation asks us to discard the false human body and mind because it is not possible to live forever with them, and to be reborn with the eternal body and mind of the Universe that never dies and never changes. Religion exists only for a person who is incomplete; it does not exist for anyone who has become complete.

Maum Meditation is about becoming a person of great freedom. In Maum Meditation, one can be reborn with the real body and mind of the Universe and Truth by discarding his human body and mind. Therefore it is where one can transcend religion and achieve human completion. It is the place where one can become a master of the true world.

The Way Forward For Man

Wanting to live the good life, a life of comfort, is the desire and state of mind of people currently living in the world. They live for this purpose but the further they go down this path, the more hopeless and wretched they become. This kind of life only brings suffering and burden.

Man suffers because he tries to make the world adjust to him. He does this because he lives with a mind of the past, which is formed by storing the experiences of his life in his mind. However, this is an act of betrayal against the world. He lives in a non-existent world, which is made by copying everything in heaven and earth - the real world. He suffers because he tries to make the world and the things in the world suit him.

Although man believes he is living in the world, he is actually living in the mind he made by taking pictures of the things in the world. Man cannot live in the true world, because he lives a life of his conceptions and habits. Such a life is in itself false and a non-existent picture. It therefore follows that man's politics, learning and everything in his life are all false. He also believes in false religions and adheres to their rules.

Whether or not one's life is righteous depends on whether he looks at the world from the world's perspective or his own. Man does not exist even while he lives in the world because he does not exist in the true world. What exists in the true world exists and what does not exist in the true world does not exist. This world is true but if man does not live in this world but in a non-existent world, an illusionary picture, he himself is an illusion and a ghost.

Man becomes righteous only when he destroys this picture world and is reborn in the true world. Only when he is born in this world will he stop speaking about illusions and instead speak of Truth. Then he will live a life without conflict, a life of universal order. He will have no self and live harmoniously with the people of the world.

This is *haewonsangsaeng* - the resolution of all human bitterness and regret and living for others - and this is the only way to love one's enemies, have great wisdom and great freedom and liberation. This is the only way to live in the complete world.

The Reason Man Is False

In the world, there is that which is true and that which is false. The world is true and man is false. He is false because he does not live in the world but inside his mind. This overlaps the world which leads him to believe he is living in the real world but actually, he is living inside a world of his mind - an illusionary world. Therefore, the world he lives in and he himself living in that world are both false.

The world just exists but your mind world is false because it does not exist. The thought that you are alive is the thought of a false ghost, and you are in a non-existent world.

You do not exist either. The true world does not disappear no matter how much you get rid of it, but falseness does. Therefore, from the perspective of Truth, it does not exist. In order to not disappear, you must be reborn from Truth.

Maum Meditation Makes That Which Does Not Exist In The World Exist

Maum Meditation was founded over ten years ago, and in that time it has made remarkable progress without too much difficulty. This was possible because what has been spoken of in many scriptures - that one must be "poor in spirit" and that one must empty and cleanse his mind - is actually being carried out in Maum Meditation.

People do not know what the mind is exactly or which minds they have to cleanse, and religions have been unable to give clarification on these questions. Maum Meditation tells us that man is false and that he can be reborn with the true body and mind of the Universe when he cleanses his sinful body and mind. It asks us to be reborn in the land of immortals by becoming Truth. One becomes Truth when none of his mind and self exist and he is reborn as the true body and mind of the Universe.

From his childhood, man's mind takes pictures through his eyes, nose, ears, mouth and body. He lives in these pictures, a video, that is an illusionary world. This is the reason people believe they live in the real world, but they are actually living in an illusionary world because each person lives in his mind, a picture world overlapping the real world. He is dead because he lives in a non-existent, illusionary picture world.

Man lives without knowing whether he is alive or dead because he does not have wisdom and he does not know what is right and real. He lives trapped inside his mind insisting only his experiences and his own thoughts are correct. Sin and karma is man's mind and man himself - this is falseness, sin and karma.

What is real is the world. The world that the Creator created is complete but man is unable to live in the world and lives instead in a world he made, an illusionary picture world that has copied the things in the world. Therefore man needs to cleanse his mind and live in the real world. The achievement of this is human completion.

Maum Meditation makes happen that which until now was only spoken of - people's minds and selves are being reborn with the body and mind of the Universe and countless saints, sages, divine-beings and buddhas are being made. This is possible at Maum Meditation because it has a method.

The world the Creator created does not lack for anything and it is completeness itself. The great Universe, the Creator, existed before the beginning and is an existence that will exist for an eternity after as it is. This existence is alive as a metaphysical real existence and its Soul and Spirit are one. When one sees from the viewpoint of this existence, the infinite Universe, all creations and this existence are one.

The world is complete because it is already born in this land of heaven. This is why it is said the world is already enlightened, but man has turned his back on the real world and instead has his own mind world. One must destroy this mind world in order to be reborn and resurrected in the world.

Only a person who is born in the real world while he is alive lives in heaven during his lifetime and after death. Maum Meditation is about changing one's false body and mind to the real body and mind of the Universe so that one can become what we have only dreamed of - he can become true and real, and live in heaven where only Truth lives while he is alive.

Perhaps this is the reason Maum Meditation continues to grow.

What Is Life?

What we think of as being alive or dead is usually judged by a certain criteria, such as whether or not it moves or fulfills a certain role. These things (that move or fulfill a certain role) live by recharging themselves with energy. For example, people live by getting energy from the food they eat, and if they do not eat, they die. Is there a way for people to live forever?

To live eternally, one must be resurrected into the Energy and God of the Universe. Before all of creation came into being, the Universe would have been just the sky: the state of completely empty space. The celestial bodies appeared in this place where there is nothing but the sky. The master of heaven and earth's creations is this existence. This existence is Truth and it is the origin and source of heaven and earth; it is an existence that is alive and the mother and father of all creation. Only this existence is Truth - the everlasting and never-dying body and mind.

The reason man has religion and so many other spiritual institutions, is because he is imperfect and incomplete. He needs religion and other organizations in order to be able to approach the complete existence that is Truth. The body is born into the world for a limited amount of time and then disappears, but one will be able to live forever without death if he is reborn while he is living as the body and mind of this existence, namely the Soul and Spirit of the Universe that is Truth.

He who becomes one with the world of the Universe's Soul and Spirit that is Truth while he is living is also Truth and thus, lives forever. The way to become reborn is to destroy one's false, imperfect and incomplete body and mind. Once he is resurrected as the existence of Truth - God and Spirit - he does not die for he is an eternal immortal that is Truth and life. The place where this process is actually carried out is Maum Meditation.

In the past many people died because hospitals and medicine did not yet exist. These days, people have access to such privileges and are able to live a longer life. Likewise, there may not have been a method to become Truth and live eternally in the past, but it is now possible because such a method exists. Only the rebirth of one's self as the body and mind of the true existence itself is the way to live forever in the land of Truth. Only this is the real life source of Truth.

Resurrection

To live after being reborn is resurrection.

There are many differing opinions about resurrection among the many sects of Christianity.

Some say one will live with this body, right here in this place, in this world while some say our bodies will change. Others believe it is the soul that lives forever.

Jesus Christ was resurrected three days after his death and lived in this world before he ascended to heaven.

No material form, from the countless different forms that exist to the human body, can exist forever.

According to scientists, the stars in the sky have life-spans that range between fifteen to forty-five billion years. The human body has an average lifespan of seventy to eighty years.

Just as a silkworm inside a cocoon must die before it can become a moth, man's body must disappear before it can be reborn as the body and mind of Truth - this is what resurrection is.

In the world, there is the origin.

In order to build a house, the ground must exist. It is because the origin exists that it is possible for all the various forms in the world to exist. The celestial bodies in the sky came forth from this origin - the original foundation - as did all creations. The law of the material world is that all material things in the world come into existence and then disappear.

From the perspective of the great Universe, there have been countless animals, plants, people and other material things on Earth that have come and gone. Their forms completely disappeared after rotting away. All of them returned to the original foundation. The Korean euphemism for death, "he has returned" means the dead have returned to the original foundation.

It is the natural order of the Universe that all the innumerable forms in the world return to nature once their forms disappear.

But man lives in a self-centered mind world, a world of illusion, so when he dies he continues on in that illusionary non-existent world. This world is hell.

Human completion is resurrection. One's body and the world of his mind must disappear to be able to return back to nature, and one must be born again with the eternally never-changing body and mind of Truth - only then is it true resurrection. One must be made of gold to go the Golden World and in the same way, one must be reborn as the substance of Truth if he is to go the land of Truth.

Christianity and Buddhism tell us that the body is a temple and a sanctuary.

This means the body itself is Truth and the origin. Only he whose self has disappeared and returned to the true origin can be resurrected in that world.

The true origin is resurrected of and by itself, but no man can live unless he is resurrected by the words of the true origin. The true origin will only allow those who have become Truth, that is, those who have returned to the origin, to live in the origin - the land of Truth.

Man can live forever only when he completely destroys his self and his delusional world and returns to the origin which is Truth, so that while he is living, the holy body and mind of Truth is resurrected within him - within the temple and sanctuary.

The body must return to great nature, and one's soul must be resurrected within great nature while he is living in order to have eternal life.

It is not man's body and mind that lives forever. Man's body and mind must die completely without anything remaining, and he must become the origin. He must be resurrected as the substance, the essence, of Truth. It is this Soul and Spirit that lives within himself for eternity.

The place we must go is the land of Truth within ourselves, and the land where we must live is also this land of Truth that exists within us.

Being born with the Soul and Spirit of Truth in the land of Truth within you is resurrection.

To Be Holy Or Divine

Although the place of God and Soul is the place where absolutely nothing exists, the existence of God and Soul does exist. The place of God and Soul is divine or holy because they exist. Truth - God and Soul - is divine because God and Soul exist amidst absolute nothingness.

We often use the word divine or holy when we see something for the first time or when we see something that is rare. However the words *divine* or *holy* mean to be like, or the same as, God and Soul.

The Meaning Of A High Level Of *Dō*

People in the world generally believe that a person has achieved a high level of *dō* if he speaks as though he knows extraordinary things or if he is able to do things that ordinary people cannot do.

The meaning of *dō* is Truth. One's level of *dō* - how much of Truth's strength one has - depends on the extent to which he has become Truth.

A person who has achieved a high level of *dō* is a person whose mind has become the Universe. A person who has achieved a complete level of *dō* is one who has become *dō* itself - one who has become Truth.

The Savior

Man's salvation is when his false self becomes real. In the Bible, it is said Jesus Christ will come again at the end of the world to take man to the world of heaven. This means the Savior will give birth to man's Soul and Spirit and allow him to live in heaven when his mind has become the sky that is Truth. Heaven remains when one's self does not exist. Salvation is the master of heaven allowing man to live in heaven.

Man, heaven and earth will be saved only when the Savior, *Maitreya*, comes. The existence of the Savior is the origin of all creations in the Universe - the Universe before the Universe. It is the Soul and Spirit that is omnipresent in the Universe. It is the metaphysical real entity that existed before material form. Man can be saved by this existence only when it comes in human form.

Man cannot see or hear this existence when it comes because it does not exist in his mind. It is said that this existence will come "as a thief in the night" or "hidden in a cloud" because no one will recognize it when it comes. These expressions mean people will not be able to recognize this existence.

The Age Of Addition

It is not possible to know from exactly when, but from a certain point in time the human race began to build an illusionary world in their minds by taking pictures. They stored these pictures in their minds and lived within them. This is the reason people need salvation and Savior - because they live in an illusion.

To become complete, people try to empty and cleanse their mind. This is the reason they began to practice religion and other forms of meditation. However if they keep adding to their minds and they do not clear out what they hold, they will become more burdened instead of achieving human completion.

Let us imagine that there is a scripture that is a thousand times better than the scriptures that exist presently. If it was taught to the people in South America or Africa for a hundred years, would those people change? As long as they have their own human minds, they would not be able to have the mind of great love or compassion. But if someone goes to South America or Africa with the method to eliminate the human mind, the people will all become Truth as long as they destroy all of their human minds. The age of incompletion was one of man ever-adding to his mind, but the time of completion is a time of subtracting the human mind. If one's human mind is completely eliminated, it is possible to be reborn with the mind of God in the land of God.

Not Even The Affairs Of The Human World Can Be Successfully Achieved With The Human Mind

A person comes to have regrets when he fails to achieve something or when he is unable to do something he wants. No matter what he achieves or gains, it is meaningless because man's very existence is a dream and an illusion. He is non-existent.

A person who lives with the thought that he must earn money becomes a slave of money. This very thought hinders him from earning money.

If he does not have such thoughts, he will become free. This does not mean he will not be able to earn any money because reality is not brought about by delusional thoughts and minds. Causes bring about results - money is earned by one's actions and not by his thoughts.

One cannot love his enemies just because he is told to do so, even if he is told numerous times. This is only possible when enemies do not exist in his mind.

All people in the world live with greed, so they want to live according to their own will. However they are unable to do so because their will is not supported by their actions. They live worrying about various things, but these worries are falseness itself. They are meaningless and they do not prevent events from happening.

It is the way of the world that cause brings effect, and that one reaps what he sows. Worries do not disappear just because one is told not to worry; they disappear when the mind of worry is discarded. It is then that things will happen according to the natural order of the Universe. A person who has done this will be able to live a better life because he will be realistic instead of having overblown dreams.

I have seen many stories on the news of wealthy people who committed suicide after losing their fortune. Many people also killed themselves when their lovers left them. These people's minds were so filled with money or love that they were unable to bear it when these things disappeared. They would have been fine if they had not had money or love in their mind. Living in the world according to universal order means one becomes the mind of the world and that he does not have human minds. If he is then born in the world, he will live well because he will be realistic.

The Work Of Maum Meditation

People frequently ask if Maum Meditation is a religion.

Maum Meditation is what its name literally states: it is a place where you cleanse your mind that is false and become reborn with the mind of Truth.

The human mind world is a place where one takes pictures of everything that belongs to the world which he stores in his mind. Man lives in this picture - the picture world - instead of living in the true world. His self living in this picture world does not exist because he is in a non-existent world. Everything in the mind disappears when you eliminate it and what disappears is false. This is the reason it needs to be cleansed.

Man can become complete only when he cleanses this mind and is reborn with the mind of Truth that does not disappear - the mind of the Creator of the origin.

In man's mind, he stores pictures of what happens in the world - pictures taken through his eyes, nose, ears, mouth and body. He does not realize he is living in a picture world and believes himself to be living in the real world because the pictures overlap the real world.

All religions ask us to cleanse and empty our minds because it is when only Truth, the origin, remains, that man can be reborn from this place and become complete. Truth remains when one's false mind world and his self living in that world are discarded.

Maum Meditation is the place where you are resurrected as your true self, after discarding your false mind world and yourself living in that world.

A person who has been reborn will live and work for the land of Truth.

Maum Meditation has the method to completely discard your false self.

If the age of incompletion was a time of storing the pictures of what you saw and heard in your mind, it is now the age of completion: a time of subtracting the picture world in your mind.

The more you add to your mind, the further you get from completion. The way to return to Truth, our deepest roots, and to become complete is to discard your self and your illusionary mind world. This is why Maum Meditation, a place to cleanse your mind, is needed. The more your mind world, that is tied to yourself, moves towards the origin and Truth, the more you will know and be enlightened.

Man who is inside his mind world mistakenly believes he is alive. In fact, he is dead because he has made an illusionary self which he believes to exist in the illusionary picture world.

What is alive is the eternal never-changing Truth. Truth, which is the world before the world and the sky before the sky, is what is alive.

Man can live forever only when he destroys his world that he made by copying Truth - the illusionary mind world - and is resurrected in the land of Truth.

Maum Meditation is the place where one discards his self and his mind world, and becomes resurrected with the body and mind of Truth that is real. This is the work of Maum Meditation.

When falseness is discarded, what is real remains. This is human completion, and it is the way to live eternally and be born in heaven while one is living. One who is born in this land will live and work in this land.

Maum Meditation is the place where you become complete. Religions are places where you talk of completion; Maum Meditation is the place where you become complete. A person who has become complete will work for the true world.

Man can live forever only when he [illegible] world [illegible] by [illegible] [illegible] world [illegible] the land of Truth.

Mount Meditation is the place where man [illegible] [illegible] world and therefore [illegible] [illegible] Truth, the real. [illegible] Mount Meditation.

When [illegible] is [illegible] [illegible]. This is [illegible] [illegible] the way to [illegible] eternity and be born in Heaven while one is alive. [illegible] [illegible] world.

[illegible] [illegible] complete. [illegible] [illegible] places [illegible] [illegible] [illegible] complete [illegible] [illegible] still [illegible] world.

Part 3

The world is an existence where
absolutely everything is alive.
When you become the world,
when you become one with the world,
you will find that everything is alive.

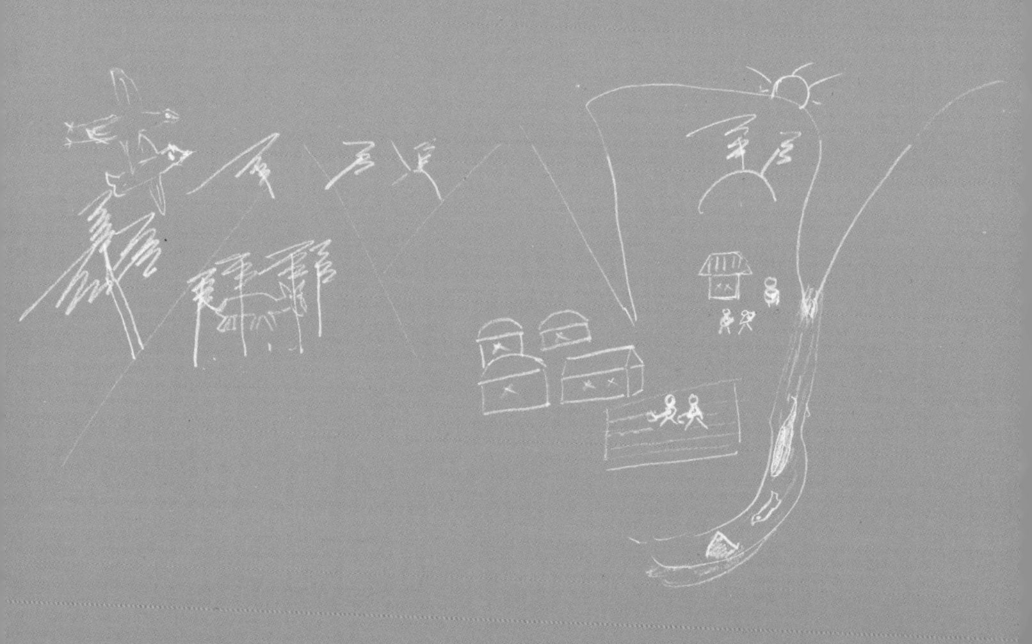

The Frailty Of Human Life

When dusk approaches on a cold day,
a person with somewhere to go does not worry
but someone who has nowhere to go worries deeply.
If he cannot find anywhere to go,
he will give up and look for any place to sleep
while worrying about how not to freeze.
A roaming wanderer will just roam, without thinking.
People and everything in the Universe live according to their environment,
and then pass away in vain.
Man lives according to human delusions
and then disappears somewhere;
like smoke or fog, he vanishes in vain.
But there were no solutions -
I mean there has been no way to just exist and just live.
Man blames life for being futile,
but those who know life's futility are those with a little sense,
while those without a clue perhaps have no sense at all.

One may ask the blue sky,
but his words do not reach it
because the sky is hidden by the cloud of the human mind.
For certain, the silent sky knows the answer, and the earth knows,
but man does not know
because no man is one with the mind of the sky and earth.
He accepts this state as fate that is not fate,
and dies without having anything to blame.
The answer is, for sure,
in the mind of the person
who has become one with the sky and earth.
I mean, he will know the futility of death
and he will have the solution to live.

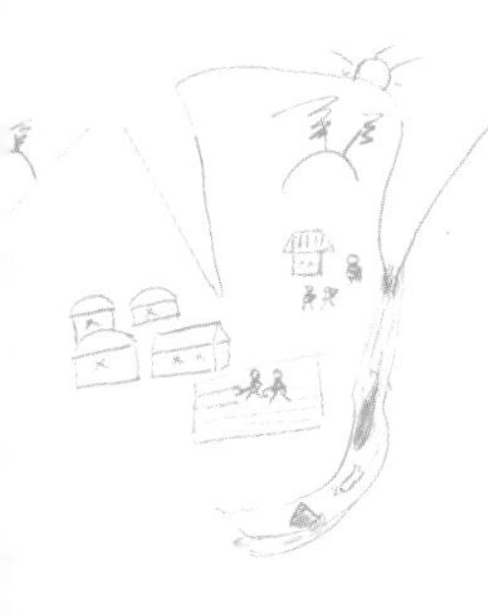

A Picture

In the darkness of night,
nothing can be seen.
Likewise, a person who lives within his sins and karma -
his mind world - does not know the ways of the world.
Just as it is possible to see the world clearly
in the bright light of day,
man can know the world
only when the true world exists in his mind.
Man, your mind is so ignorant -
was there so little to eat,
that you ate picture scraps?
You do not know they are false, and not real,
because you are inside a picture,
and can only see the world of pictures.
If you see from the world,
they are all false.

What is real is the world;

what is real is the living world;

what is real is the true world.

Only man does not live in the world

but takes pictures of the world,

stores them in his mind,

and lives within them.

Salvation is escaping from this world

and being resurrected in the true world.

Man lives with the delusion he is living in the world,

because his mind world overlaps the real world.

Inside a video of past memories,

he is groaning with pain, suffering

and there, ageing, sickness, birth and death exist.

Inside a video,

he lives bound within its framework;

he cannot rest for he is not free.

Sighing, he re-lives the shadows of past memories,

believing that those shadows are him,

and he lives speaking the nonsense of pictures.

Those who know this are wise,

but those who do not know do not understand

because they cannot hear the words of the world

from within the video.

It is unlikely that a dead person, an illusionary person,

who is inside a video would be able to hear the words of Truth.

He jabbers on without knowing the true meaning or purpose,
but his words are all lies and nonsense.
So close your mouth,
and concentrate on cleansing your sins and karma
by discarding, then discarding again.
You may speak the nonsense of picture scraps,
but they are just the sounds of a ghost,
so just keep discarding
for then you will be able to hear the words of Truth,
and speak words of Truth.
Do not walk around speaking lies and doing false deeds,
but be born from Truth
so that you may live for the world, and speak true words.
You should learn to listen to words of Truth.

Nature's Flow

A wanderer who has turned against the world
does not have anywhere to go.
He lives inside his mind, with burdens, sufferings and agonies.
By living a life against the ways of the world,
he is trapped inside a grave.
When a person of the world listens to the chattering of ghosts
who are each inside the graves of their own greatness,
he finds they do not acknowledge each other,
and only speak about themselves.
They all want to be acknowledged -
their stories are all of how great they are,
asking you to come into their worlds.
None of their stories are of any use,
all of them are lies, and more lies.
Man steals what belongs to the world while living in the world,
and having forsaken the mind of thankfulness to the world,
the existence of which allows all creations to exist,
he makes his own world, duplicated from the real world.

It becomes a false world,
and because he has turned away from the true world,
it is death.
His outer form may resemble a human-being,
but he is not a person, he is a ghost.
A ghost is an illusion,
and a ghost believes his self exists,
but a person who has come to his senses
can see that a ghost does not exist.
Ghosts are afraid of ghosts and do not trust other ghosts.
There is an old saying, that when walking in a deep forest,
it is not the animals or ghosts that you should be afraid of,
but people.
This means people are ghosts,
and it is people who harm other people.
One who has turned his back on the world
will die and become a ghost.
He has nowhere to go
because he has turned away from the world;
he will end up dying eternally
because he has turned away from the world.
Know the true meaning of these words,
and come back to the world and live.
There is no world outside of the world,
and there is nowhere to live outside of the world.

There is nowhere to live, for there the world does not exist.
The world you stole as you pleased is not the world,
it is a place where ghosts live;
it is the world of ghosts, and ghosts themselves
are of a non-existent world, so it is death.
Come back, lost child, to the world!
Live according to the ways of the world,
and live in a world of nature's flow.
All things happen according to their conditions -
there is not one thing that happens
according to the nonsensical thoughts of a ghost.

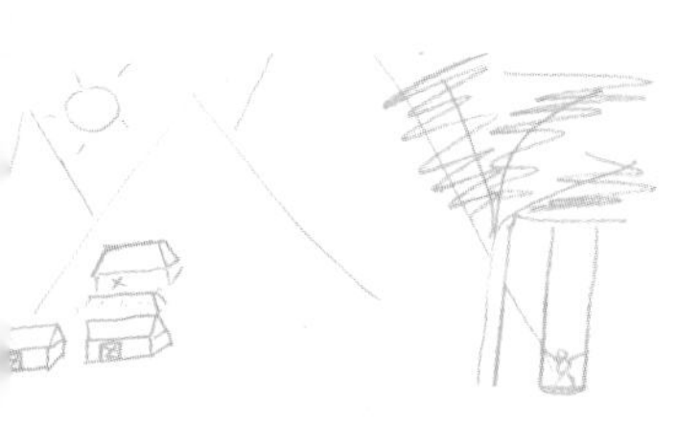

Truth And Falseness II

Truth is what is living and falseness is what is dead,
it is what exists and what does not exist.
If it exists in the world, it is Truth,
and if it does not, it is falseness.
The former is eternally alive,
and the latter does not live, because it does not exist.
If it exists in the world, it exists
but if it does not, then it does not exist.
What exists in the world exists,
and what does not exist in the world, does not.
The countless stories of man do not exist
because they do not exist in the world,
and what is not in accordance with the ways of the world
do not exist in the world.
A person who has achieved everything
is he who has been born in the complete world,
and a person who has not achieved
is he who has not been born in the complete world.

One's soul must be born again as the Soul of the Universe

in order to live, and not die.

Ignorant Of Truth's Will

Just as a sparrow does not know the will of a phoenix,
and animals do not know the will of people,
a person living in a false world
does not know the will of a person of the true world.
He does not know falseness or Truth,
existence or non-existence;
he does not know the world or his own non-existent world.
Man is false.
While there is no Truth in man,
a person who knows he is false will strive to become true.
It is the will of a true person
to make what is false become true,
but man does not know what falseness and Truth are;
he is an illusion that speaks only of himself within himself.
How can a ghost know the will of a true person,
which is to make ghosts into God,
and make falseness live as Truth?

A Limited Time

The day is getting dark,
and a cold early winter draws near.
Spring, summer and fall have passed, as they always do -
isn't life colorful?
There was a time when it was hard to get through the cold winter
because of the longings and regrets remaining in my mind;
the difficult life of the past became a jinx, and I was lonely.
My regrets, from the time that passed silently and meaninglessly,
come from the things I could not achieve from countless events.
But that time does not return,
and youth does not return.
While people may long for their old memories,
I do not find them beautiful.
Perhaps it is because of the bitterness that comes from
not having been able to do the things I wanted to do,
or have the things I wanted to have.
Times passes meaninglessly and it passes silently,
but what is for certain,

is that the events from those days of long ago
do not return.
Here in America, where I am currently,
there are many who left their homelands with their memories.
They emigrated in order to find a better life.
There are people here from many countries -
North and South America, Africa, Europe, the Middle East, Australia, New Zealand, China, Russia, Uzbekistan, and so on who left their home countries, holding onto their memories of them; there are some who died here on foreign soil without being able to go back, and there are the third and fourth generations of those who came during the first wave of immigrants, who are still living on foreign soil.
The Koreans here have little knowledge of Korea, and cannot speak Korean;
they have adjusted to living in this one part of Earth.
Regardless of where they live,
we are all compatriots,
but then again, we are not really.
We are neither on the same wavelength,
nor can we communicate with each other.
Since we look alike, we glance at each other as we pass,
and that is all - it is a pity.
They have forgotten Korea, their motherland,
and even their religion is not Korean, but someone else's.

Naturally over the course of time, their ethnicity is slowly disappearing.
When completion, the great path, spreads all over the world,
the world will become one.
It is for that day,
that I have become a traveler of the world,
roaming,
and roaming again.
Just as there are places of light when there are places of shade,
there will come a day when light comes into the shade.

A Virtuous Person Has Nowhere In The World To Rest

Under which sky, in which country,
is there a place for me to rest?
There are many countries and places in the world,
but there is nowhere for me to rest,
and nowhere can I speak openly of the Truth.
In which country, and under which sky
do true freedom and peace exist?
Only great nature is one with my mind, and exists silently
but the world is so completely false,
that for someone such as me
who teaches people they are false
and gives them new birth as Truth,
it is not just a place of rest that is the issue,
but that I cannot openly teach my message.
Great nature, that is silent, is one with me
and it is on my side,
but in the world there are only wolves in sheep's clothing
beckoning from a dark and non-existent place

to come into their worlds.
If something does not suit their frame of mind,
they are cold and even take lives,
and although it cannot be seen with the eyes,
a wolf is a ghost who asks others to live by its rules.
Even though it is told that such a world is not right
it thinks that what it is doing is the most correct.
The world is filled with wolf packs,
with ghosts, in sheep's clothing.
A world where one either eats or is eaten
has continued for thousands, tens of thousands of years,
but in such a world,
does a place of true freedom and peace for man exist?
The land must be stripped of the wolves' clothing,
and the wolves - the ghosts - must die and be reborn
and become one with the mind of the true world,
for only then can they live in the complete world created by the Maker.
But wolves, telling the stories of countless events,
are living in the lap of luxury, and for their own benefit,
they mask themselves in sheep's clothing
while eventually feeding on others.
Just as Jesus Christ told us,
the mountain creatures and birds all have homes,
but there is nowhere in the world

for a virtuous person to rest.
Politics, economics and religions, none have a perfect plan;
so, even the Soviet Union collapsed.
Many countries under this system have fallen,
subsisting quietly for awhile while under the governance of a competent person,
then eventually crumbling.
The economy also does well for a time before failing,
recovers, then fails again.
Religions are not able to become one with the words of past saints -
they may speak of their words,
but their minds are that of pictures, of ghosts.
To argue that one is right when he is not Truth
and there is not one iota of Truth in him,
is foolishness amongst foolishness,
yet no one even realizes that this is foolish.
The plan to live well, with true peace, freedom and equality,
the plan for man to live happily and forever,
is to get rid of pictures - to get rid of the world of the mind.
The problem is man only hears what he already knows,
and furthermore, he does not even try to listen.
He who is trapped inside a grave,
can only spout stories of the grave
but for someone who lives in the world
they are stories of rotting corpses,

the sounds of gas emitting from shit-filled graves.
All around, there are only sounds of rotting,
the sounds of boiling shit,
so a living person cannot speak
and there is nowhere for him to rest;
at a loss, he waits.
Without the ghosts knowing, he moves.

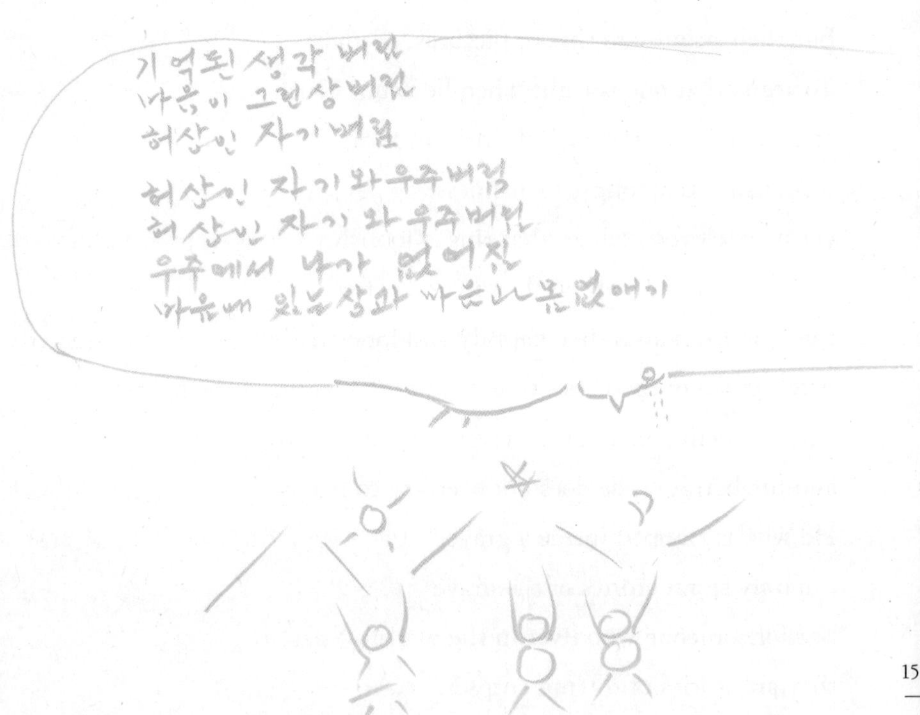

Maum Meditation Is About Discarding Everything, Not Having More

Often, many people come to Maum Meditation,
and just as they have always done in their worldly lives,
they want their selves to become enlightened,
to know something and to become complete.
Some do the meditation
to improve and better their false selves,
to be idolized,
or to become leaders of some false religious cult.
Those who meditated with the purpose of gaining power over others strove to achieve their goal,
but failed because the aims of the meditation were far removed from theirs.
They left, and many wandered in the wrong places,
before coming back eventually.
Maum Meditation is a place where you throw away the false picture world - the human mind world -
and your very self that lives in the false picture.
What this means and what it asks us to do

is to discard our human bodies and minds,
and change to the body and mind of the Universe.
It asks us to eliminate all of our bodies and minds from the Universe
so that we may be reborn with the body and mind of the true living
God - the Universe.
It asks us to become Truth itself -
the eternal and never-changing body and mind of the Universe.
When one's false self disappears from the Universe,
isn't the true world the only thing remaining?
He who is born in this world is a saint and a child of God.
It is when one is reborn in the everlasting land of God
that one becomes a living person.
If you just subtract yourself from the world,
the true world remains
and you will be born in the true world
and live forever.
Maum Meditation is the place where one's false self is discarded
and he becomes reborn as what is real in the world that is real.
It is the place where you throw away your false body and mind.

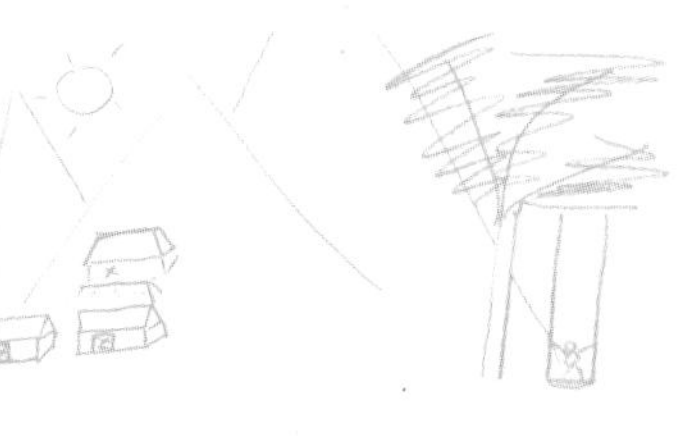

The Past, Present And Future, Good, Bad, Burdens And Sufferings Exist In the False Ghost World Where Man Lives, But None Of These Things Exist In God's World

We have often heard,
that human life itself is an illusion,
that we live in a delusion,
and that someday the Savior will come to save us.
Religions tell us to cleanse and empty our minds
because we do not live in a righteous world.
Man believes he lives in the true world
but the world he lives in overlaps the real world.
He is living in a film, a movie that he himself has made.
From a young age, he makes a film
which he keeps inside his mind -
he lives inside this film of pictures taken of the world.
Think about the breakfast that you had this morning:
the place where you were sitting and what you ate
were taken as pictures inside your mind;
it is not what happened in the world
but it was in a picture, in your mind.
The breakfast you ate and what you did all day,

aren't they all inside that film, in your mind?

You were not inside the world,

but inside your mind,

and even this moment, if you think about it once it has passed,

isn't it also in a picture?

The world and this moment is overlapping inside the mind

so man believes that he is living in the world.

If he becomes one with the world, and lives in the world,

he will not have any pictures.

The human mind is a film that takes and stores pictures

but the mind of the world does not take pictures.

Man does not know this

so he is not born in the world

and he is not saved.

There is suffering, burden, life, death, good, bad,

ageing, sickness, birth, death, the past, the future and the present

in the world of these pictures;

but when you become one with the true world

and you are born in the world,

these things do not exist;

it is eternal, never-changing life itself.

When Will The Messiah Come?

Many people believe the Messiah -
Christ who was crucified two thousand years ago -
is somewhere up in heaven and will come down on a cloud
with trumpeting angels to save us.
It is also written so in the Bible,
but the term *Christ* refers to the true existence
who has become one with the Creator and Truth.
In other words, it refers to a person who is real and alive.
What it means when it says that Christ will come again,
is that the existence of Truth will come -
for then the Messiah has come.
Salvation is changing a false man into Truth.
Even when Truth comes to the world,
man will not recognize Truth for he only sees the outer form
and he does not have any Truth in him.
This is why it is said man does not know anything.
Man who is inside his mind world only knows what is in his world
and he does not know the principles of the true world.

The meaning of "the Messiah will come hidden on a cloud"
is people who live in their mind worlds
will not know when Truth comes or goes;
they have no Truth within them,
so even when the true Christ, Truth, comes
they will not know.
Man who does not live in the true world
does not know the true meaning of the Bible,
the Buddhist scriptures or any of the other scriptures.
Christ who is Truth, does not dwell in a form or shape -
when man becomes Truth,
Christ who is Truth, has come.
The salvation of man
is falseness becoming Truth;
it is being born in the real world from the false world.
Christ who is real must come,
for only he can make man become Truth.

The Reason Man Cannot See Truth Or Know Truth

Man does not know anything about the world of Truth,
because he does not live in the world.
Instead, he lives in his mind world - a copy of the world.
The Bible and Buddhist scriptures were spoken from the true world
but since they are read from within people's minds,
they are interpreted differently depending on what their minds hold.
This is the reason there are so many different religious sects.
Man is living in a mind world overlapping the world,
so he lives not in the world but in his mind
and thus, he does not know the world of Truth.
He must become one with the world
in order to know it and see it.
The reason he is unable to see the world of Truth
is the world of Truth does not exist in man's mind.
Only a person who has been resurrected as Truth
can know Truth and see Truth.
Truth is the world,

and when man becomes the world,

and he is reborn in the world,

he can know the ways of the world.

Being Truth, death will not exist for him.

Enlightenment

Enlightenment is what one comes to know,
when he comes out from his false mind world
and he becomes Truth -
which happens to the extent of how much falseness he has discarded.
Truth emerges as much as one has been absolved of his sin and karma,
and what he comes to know in the moment of realization,
is enlightenment.
When the Bible tells us to believe with the heart,
and confess with the mouth,
it is speaking of enlightenment.
From the starting point of knowing nothing,
man will come to know and be enlightened of many things
along the way to becoming Truth.

A Lifetime

Everyone lives a human lifetime, then dies.
A human lifetime is seventy to eighty years
whereas the lifetime of the Universe is eternity.
Everything born in the Universe,
lives as long as the age of the Universe.
Man does not know how to live as long as the age of the Universe,
because he does not have wisdom.
If you become one with the true world,
you will be born in the world and live there.
A Soul and Spirit born in the world does not die.
The Soul and Spirit of Truth just lives, forever and ever.
When the Universe - the Creator and source of the world -
brought man and all creations into being,
their very existence was made by the Energy and Light of the Universe
to exist in the land of Truth eternally without death.
This is the unintended intention, the will, of the Creator.
Just living,

without worries,
without sufferings and burden,
free from all things
is deliverance, freedom and liberation.
The land that is true is the land without ageing, sickness, life and death.
This land is the land of universal order and great love.
The greed in man's mind is sin and karma
and therefore it is suffering and burden,
but for a person who amasses blessings in this land
those blessings are his
and the joy in his mind will be boundless.
Man must come into this land while he is living,
and while living, he must amass blessings.
To be alive one must be Truth -
one is only alive when he has become Truth -
so a person who has not become Truth is dead.
Do not live a human lifetime,
but live forever - live the lifetime of the Universe.

The Non-Existent World

Mankind has lived from a long time ago,
and in the millions of human lives there have been,
there has always been sadness and torment.
There is a song that says,
that even if you live your life in a mansion with lush fields,
it is nothing but a dream-like illusion when you pass away.
We live without meaning or purpose
and then die without meaning or purpose.
When we are young, we live with our parents,
running and playing with childish abandon.
Then we go to school, get married,
have children and raise them.
Time flies like an arrow
and man lives like a worm of this meaningless life -
our children leave the nest
and our hair turns gray.
As we become engrossed in life's various events and stories,
we come to have people we like and enemies.

However these stories with their countless joys and sorrows,
are all shadows of memories gone by.
We leave the world without having fulfilled anything in such lives,
which is why inside the mind worlds we made -
those shadows of memories -
we go through *samsara*, the perpetual cycle of death and rebirth.
A person who wakes from his dream is startled to find
his parents, siblings, spouse, children,
and everyone he knows are ghosts;
that he lived with ghosts in the world;
and that it was a world of ghosts.
He does not want to think or look back again.
A person who has woken,
will live as an eternal immortal
in the new world.
Ghosts end up dying
because they live in a non-existent world -
it is death.

Come Out Into The World

Man has lived through countless ages,
and within those innumerable ages,
there have been the stories and sufferings of many.
But then, as now, time does not exist,
and the world exists, just as it is, without response.
Only man's mind was busy, wanting to achieve something,
and he suffered and was burdened, trying to fulfill his will.
He did not live in accordance with universal order,
and he was not able to live in harmony with the world.
Instead, he tried to make the world adapt to him,
so his was a life that betrayed nature's flow.
Man originally lived as one with the world -
a life of universal order -
but from the moment he had the mind of greed,
the mind that contained the world within it,
he became a traitor of universal order.
Oh people, the world just exists as it is.
Heroes, stories, and all the other innumerable things man has made,

have followed the passage of time and disappeared,
but the world and the sky still just exist.
Just as the world just exists
while all that man has made and possessed have disappeared,
one who is born in the world,
will live with the Soul that has become one with Truth,
as long as the age of the world.
Even though man lives, he is not really living
for he has dug his own grave, that is his mind world.
From inside the grave, he constructs it ever more strongly,
continuously building and building.
Isn't he therefore, dead?
From the viewpoint of the world,
both the grave and one's self inside the grave,
are non-existent illusions.
If your grave and self do not exist,
you can come out into the world,
and live as one with the world.
Then, time, that flows as water flows, does not exist
and you are the Soul of the world;
you are Truth, and without death.
Come out, into the world!
Everything that is yours is all useless illusions and hell,
so destroy the world of hell
and come out into the world.

If It Is Not Truth And Real, It Is False

No one, among men, knows what is real or what is false.
No one, among men, knows Truth or falseness.
Only when man becomes real and complete,
is he actually real.
What is real is the world,
and what is false is man.
Man has copied the world, and what belongs to the world,
and in his mind, he possessed the world and the things of the world,
and he lives making his conceptions and habits.
Thus, he is a treacherous sinner who has sinned against the world, the Creator.
Man who has conceptions and habits in his mind,
does not have anything real within him,
so he does not know what is real.
From the perspective of the world that is real,
everyone in the world are not complete,
so they are false.
The method to become real,

is to completely discard the conceptions and habits
of man who is false.
If man does not become real,
he is completely false.
If you are practicing a faith or attending a place
but you have not become complete and real,
it is false.
There is nothing real in the world man lives in,
and a real person does not exist.
A person who has eliminated the false world and his false self,
is reborn in the world that is real, and becomes real.
That is, he achieves human completion.
If one has not become Truth and real now,
isn't everything all false?
Paradise and eternal heaven
is a place where only one who has become complete,
he who has become real, can go.
To say that you will go to heaven after death
makes no sense.
It is only when you are real while you are living,
that you can go to the land that is real.
You must be Truth to go to the land of Truth,
for what is false does not exist.
In the past, people could only walk or run
but now, there are cars and planes -

Similarly, people think human completion
is something that can only be done by saints,
like Jesus, Shakyamuni or Mohammed,
but just as there are now cars and planes,
won't there be a point in time when man can become complete?
An incomplete being is always incomplete
even if it tries to become complete,
but when the incomplete being is completely destroyed
Truth remains.
When you are reborn from Truth,
you will become complete.

The Meaningless Stories Of Life

Over in the far side of the open field,
the river flows silently.
Holding the stories of joys and sorrows,
the river and the water exist,
but the stories only exist within the thoughts
of the people that hear them.
Within those stories of sorrow,
they would have had similar thoughts to mine.
In the mountains, birds are chirping,
river-birds are flying by the riverside,
and at night, a wolf howls and an owl hoots.
Pheasants and squirrels that dart around looking for food during the
day are all asleep,
as are the mountain birds and creatures.
From the depths of the mountains,
the sound of the temple bells rings my heart.
Those bells must have rung out for hundreds of years without fail,
but no traces of the many people who have lived here remain.

People lived ignorant of the meaning and purpose of their birth,
and passed away after living a lifetime of seventy-odd years.
Their stories may have been passed down,
but there is no trace of them -
they are all dreams that have drifted by.
All those who lived this meaningless life with greed,
those who dominated over the world,
those who robbed and were robbed -
they have all disappeared.
The smoke of dinner cooking rises from the chimneys of every house
in the village,
and farmers are hurriedly finishing up their work.
Those who have returned from the fields gather at the inn
to drink a bowl of *makgeolli* before heading home.
They chat with their families over the evening meal,
and as night falls, the rowdy chirping of crickets
mirrors the villagers' gossip.
The families, the villagers, live oblivious of many things -
the meaning of life, and what it is to live -
They are focused only on how to possess things in their present
lives.
It is while they are trying to live better lives,
that they die holding onto their sorrowful stories.
When a drunken husband passes away,
his wife cries relentlessly despite all the trouble he gave her

because of the strong brand of affection
that comes from a mixture of love and hate.
All people each have their own stories,
etched into their numerous minds.
Even now, after much time has passed,
people live in an illusion, a world of ghosts.
The neighbors, villagers, parents, siblings, spouses and children - everyone - were all ghosts.
From the viewpoint of the world, man is a non-existent entity that lives in a non-existent world - namely, man is a ghost.
Stories and histories are all tales of ghosts.
Ghosts disappear but nature remains.
The sky that is great nature, just exists, without changing,
and if man became one with the world of great nature,
he would live there as an eternally living immortal,
but man, who tries to make everything his, disappears completely.
The reason and purpose man is born into the world
is to become one with the world,
and to be born in the world.
Those who build towers in the world of ghosts are foolish,
and those who amass blessings in the world are wise.
When there is nothing that is yours in all that you have and own,
in not possessing, you can find what is truly yours.
Man does not know whether he is living or dead,
and he tries hard to possess things,

but everything he has is false,

because all things do not exist.

When there is nothing that is mine,

there is what is truly mine.

A Life Of Nature's Flow

Nature is so plentiful -

if it lives without any particular hardships,

it is because of God's protection.

Nature does not speak, but it is created and lives

of and by itself, by the conditions of nature.

Everything in the world is cause and effect.

In the world, *this* exists because *that* exists,

and it is through the harmony and balance of this and that

that all creations are made.

Creation happens only when the conditions for creation exist -

if the conditions are the cause, what is created is the effect.

In the world, *this* exists because *that* exists,

and it is because various people exist, that I can exist.

The reason man finds life difficult,

is he tries to live according to his own will.

When he lays down all that is in his mind,

becomes one with the world and adapts to the world,

it will not be so difficult.

Instead of blaming the world,
if he blames and discards his own wrongful body and mind,
he will become a person who fits in the world,
and just as great nature, the world, does,
he will live a life of universal order.
Just as man cannot prevail over great nature,
which is silent, unchanging, and in accordance with universal order,
the world does not bend to man's will.
He who tries to live in the world with his will,
will just suffer needlessly.
The world, which is God,
gave us all the conditions in which to live,
but without an ounce of gratitude,
man speaks his own words, forms his own will
and lives selfishly.
He has taken great pains, needlessly,
to make his own world,
while turning his back on the true world.
If he knew the world he made is false and a picture,
he would not be able to hold his head up for shame.
Man's purpose is to be born in the world of Truth.
Even in Maum Meditation,
those who hold onto their false selves,
and try to contain Truth within their falseness
are still just false ghosts.

Only when one's self that is a ghost is completely gone,
is it possible to be reborn as a child of God.
Eliminating one's illusionary world
and being reborn, resurrected, in the world that is reality,
is the meaning and will behind Maum Meditation.

There Is No Truth In Human Conceptions And Habits

Heaven and earth is alive,
and it consists of a great Soul and Spirit.
Everything is alive,
because everything is the embodiment of the Soul and Spirit.
For man to be born and live in the world,
he must become one with the world
and live a life of the world.
Instead, man lives life
trapped in his mind.
When there is absolutely nothing in the world,
the true world exists.
But all of it is inside man's delusional mind,
so he believes that he is living in the world.

There is no *dō*, Truth, in man's conceptions and habits.
Man's words and life are limited to
what he has learned and what he knows.
He made his own world

but that itself is an illusion;
it is sin; karma; and a picture.
There is nothing right in it or about it.
All the conceptions and habits man has are illusions and pictures,
and there is nothing true or real in them.
He may speak like a saint,
or act like a saint,
but he is falseness itself
because he does not exist in the world,
though he may not know it.
None of his conceptions and habits are right.
What is real are the actions
of a person who has been born in the world -
everything he does is real.

The Living World

There is not a cloud to be seen,
and in the clear sky,
there is an endless expanse of silent stars.
Even in those days of long, long ago,
in the history of rowdy people,
they would have existed silently.
The rowdy people have been swallowed up by the years.
All creations and celestials bodies that exist under heaven,
will one day also be swallowed up by the years -
but this happens only in the world of man's mind.
If you become the world,
all things that have become one with the world are alive.

The Reason Man Cannot Live Like Flowing Water

History and the numerous different stories of the past -
images that do not exist - are in one's imagination.
People live with the countless stories that arise from their greed,
but these are all just dreams.
A dream is an illusion that does not exist, though it may seem to exist,
and just as it exists, yet at the same time it does not,
these stories are born from delusions.
Human life is born from a delusion and it is lived in a delusion.
Man tries and struggles to possess time that has already passed,
he tries to turn back time,
but it is futile.
Living in the present reality, and being in the present is *dō*.
Living out the present holding onto countless images
is burden - this is man's karma.
Although it has been said that man must just live, and just exist,
they are all just words.
Man cannot live like the flowing water
because of the pictures he has in him,

and with them he judges and discriminates what is right and wrong.
These judgments and discriminations arise from his conceptions and habits.
A tree must be a tree;
the shadow of a tree is not the tree.
Likewise, if man is living in the world,
he should live in the world and nowhere else.
Why then has he drawn and stored the world -
the shadow of the world - within him?
It is greed, from the mind of possession.
Man, who cannot hear or speak the news of the world,
does not know the true will or purpose,
and there is no one who tries to know.
Far from repenting, all people are bellowing they are great -
it is no different than a scene from a tragic play.
It is laughable to see them building and destroying castles in the air
within the plays they themselves have made.
Man is not in the world because he does not have the consciousness of the world,
but inside the play he himself wrote,
he must live like a squirrel running in his wheel;
like a character in a video, he does not have life -
an illusion is not alive; it is dead.

The World Of Divine Beings

Deep in the mountains densely studded with pine trees,
there is a lake.
The long, straight reddish pines are very appealing;
they pierce the sky, as if to boast of their height -
they would have needed a lot of time to grow so tall.
Hundreds of years old, they give off a lovely scent.
Above the lake, high up amidst the rocks,
a waterfall bursts forth and pounds its way down,
while an unidentifiable bird flies round and round high in the sky.
Gentle storks are sitting on top of the pine trees, here and there,
whiling away the day.
White clouds that dot through the clear sky
make the scene even more picturesque.
In the water, which is so blue it is almost black,
unidentifiable fish are swimming to and fro,
and once in a while this place is visited
by people who want to be companions of worry-free nature.
I follow the steep mountain path, and after a long while,

I come across an old uninhabited house
that looks like it is over a hundred years old.
I walk down the mountain thinking about who had lived there
and I see deer leisurely eating the grass.
The mountain birds chirp incessantly,
and the sound of the water is clamorous,
but the water is crystal clear.
After walking down for a long time,
I come across a place where many people live.
It is like stumbling into the *saha* world
from the world of divine beings.
The world inside my mind is the *saha* world,
and the world I am born into after becoming one with the world
is the world of divine beings.

Let's Work In The New World And Amass Blessings

Regardless of how far one walks and walks, and walks,
there is no end.
There is good and bad in the futile stories of life,
therefore there is nothing truly good in the world.
One might be busy, but he is busy in vain -
no matter what he does, he does not achieve anything,
and no matter how far he walks, he does not get anywhere.
Struggling along with the years that silently pass,
thinking only of the futile events of life,
all that he achieves, all that man's achievements amount to,
is his own protection, and the tending of his fame and security.
After struggling for my own benefit in a dream world,
I have been born in the land of light -
and I know the ways of heaven and earth,
because my eyes can now see clearly.
There is not one thing to have or take in life,
but a person who amasses treasures, blessings, in the land of Truth,
is truly wealthy.

What man needs to do while he is living,
is to be born in the world of light and Truth,
and amass many blessings by working for the true world.
Such a person is truly wise.
Time passes silently, and he who does not do so,
will struggle and bear a heavy burden.
Many people live in the latter way,
but no one realizes that they do.
The only way to know how to escape from human suffering,
is to completely die.
Just as it is only possible to see from another point of view,
when you let go of yourself and see from a third person's viewpoint,
when you die and become the standpoint of the Universe that is the world,
it is possible to see and know the world properly.
One is born in the world in order to live,
and in order to amass fortune in the true world.

Do not live a life that is futile,
but be born in the land where there is light,
where all people work for the new world;
where they work to build a rich, new world.

Part 4

Human completion is discarding one's false body and mind and being reborn with the body and mind of the origin that is real.
The pure and noble place of Truth cannot be achieved while holding onto one's self; it is in the place where one completely discards his self.

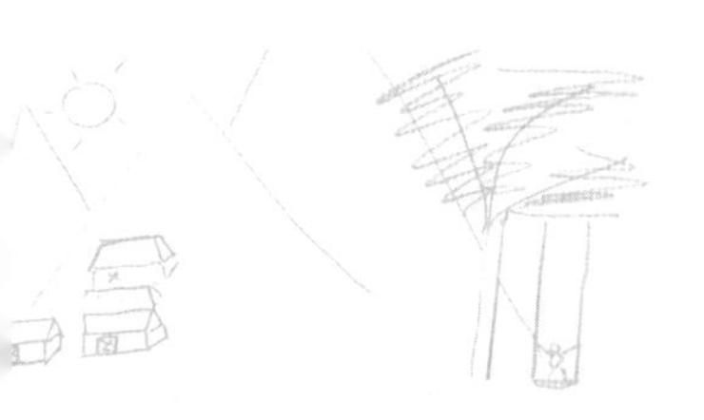

The Way To Be Born In Heaven And Live There

There is not a cloud in the endlessly high sky.
It is from here that heaven and earth were made,
and it is to this place that they return.
Man is also born from the harmony and balance of the sky and earth.
The sky is infinite and silent, but it is omniscient and omnipotent.
I am thankful to exist in the consciousness of the sky before the sky.
I am thankful to exist in the world.
Now that I have come to my original senses,
I am one with the world
and I live with the world according to universal order.
The reason people bow and pray to the heavens, the sky, is,
it is the original consciousness that fulfills all things.
Everything in the world is like the clouds in the sky,
and only the sky - the land of *Jung* and *Shin* -
is the eternal real world.
Becoming complete and alive
is being born and living in heaven,
but this path is one of discarding only.

When one's self is gone,
the consciousness of heaven remains,
and he is reborn in heaven.

Man's Fate Inside His Baggage

For the peace,
great freedom,
and abundant happiness of the world.

Heaven and earth is a world of oneness,
but man does not know its will.
He does not know the world
because he lives inside himself.
While we live, we see and hear all sorts of things,
but they are all meaningless.
A wanderer is flustered inside the burden
where he has trapped himself,
and he does not know where to go.
He bears too much burden,
and he himself is trapped in its baggage.
Unable to come out into the world from the baggage that cannot even be seen,
he lives blundering inside it,

and then eventually dies within it.
All that he has in his baggage,
are things he has stolen from the world,
but there is nothing real in pictures that have copied the world.
In a false world he lives without knowing the will and purpose of
his life,
and when he dies, he is ignorant still.
It is an eternal end, devoid of life; it is death.
The reason man lives in the world is in order to truly live,
but far from living, he is unable to forget his baggage,
and he is not able to live - this is death itself.
He is naturally extinguished along with the passage of time.
Man must die in order to know the world beyond,
but he is only concerned with the upkeep of his baggage.

The Providence Of Nature

Following the flowing river,
the river does not speak, but just calmly flows and flows;
such is the providence of nature.
It does not speak and yet it fulfills its role.
The mountains and the water each do everything they need to do,
because they live in the forms they were given
according to the will of nature, of God.
But man, who speaks too much, is burdened and suffers,
because his actions are against the universal order of nature,
and tries to make the world fit the world of his own will.
All that one needs to do is just live
in the shape and form he was given,
but he suffers because he tries to make things belong to him.
The wind is able to blow,
because of the conditions in nature that allow it to blow.

Man needs to just live according to nature's providence
but he dreams vain dreams and does meaningless things,

so he lives each day with regrets.
His mind is never satisfied,
regardless of what he achieves.
If one lives positively with the mind of the world,
it is possible for him to simply just live.
Man is not satisfied by anything he does
because he tries to satiate his mind that is a futile delusion.

Everything that exists in the world,
fulfills the role of its shape and form
and lives without its own mind.
Only man is burdened
because he lives in his mind and tries to fill it;
this is the reason he is not one with the world,
the reason he blames and disavows the world.
If he casts off these delusions and lives in the origin
there is great freedom and liberation;
there is no human suffering,
and he can live a true life.

Those Illusions···

As a bitterly cold wind blows,
a person takes leave of his beloved home and family.
He is loath to go.
But regardless of what he is leaving to do,
the reason he feels he must leave
is in order to find a better life.
For man, life is a continuous series of partings.
Of those who left their homes long ago,
countless people returned home as chilly corpses.
Only a few had the deliberate intention of success;
in search of a better life,
many left for further study
or to work in factories.
All of them left with their homes in their hearts,
keeping those homes of the past in their minds
even with the passing of the years.
The reason one misses home
is because of his childhood -

a time spent freely without responsibilities.
In all the towns and villages where there are people
each household lives with their own tales of sorrow,
because everyone lives inside his own mind,
from which they are unable to escape.
At home, all close, bosom friends have gone;
now, no such people remain,
and from time to time one may hear news
of them living in foreign places.
Home was a place where all people lived inside human minds -
it all happened inside falseness, a picture.
It was a false world.
Life is meaningless and false
because the past was lived entirely inside a picture.
In ignorance of whether Truth comes, goes, exists or not,
man lives out a futile life, at the end of which
only a grave remains.
In places where life was lived affectionately together
people, their once-generous natures, have changed.
Such places, of my memories, have disappeared
and apart from a few familiar faces,
most are strangers.
I have wandered and wandered,
searched high and low,
for a place that is good to live

but those who had fulfilled their will have vanished -
they followed the passage of time
ignorant of where they were headed.
Who knows where they went?
Those illusions…
They must all be lost still,
wandering round the illusionary world.

One Must Be The Origin In Order To Live As The True Origin

At dawn, the world and all its creations wake from their sleep
and they each do what they need to do.
What they do is not done by them,
but by the will of heaven.
All creations live of and by themselves - they just live -
and only man lives by his own will.
Man lives with hardship, suffering and burdens
because he lives by the script of the programmed human mind.

To live the way you were originally made
means to live with the mind of the Universe,
which is the form of the origin.
It means to live without any burdens by casting everything off,
thereby becoming real and Truth.
It also means to live according to universal order,
and to live with the mind of nature;
to live accepting all things, unobstructed by one's own will.
Everything in the world just lives,

but man is heavily burdened,
because he tries to live by his own will.
If the whole world lives by the providence of nature,
then anyone can be free; anyone can be liberated.
Man lives a difficult life
because he lives inside his own mind,
within which he tries to make the world fit.
He is burdened, negative, disgruntled, and suffers,
because he lives inside that mind.
Casting off that mind is the method of Maum Meditation.
Truth is when man does not exist, and he is reborn
as the body and mind of the great Universe -
the body and mind of God and nature.
No matter how he pretends to be proper, decent, good and wise,
he cannot be truly proper, decent, good or wise
unless he has become the mind of nature.
One who has not become his original form is completely false,
and cannot possibly live how he was originally made, as Truth.
To return back to one's original form is to return to the origin,
which can only happen when he discards all of his false self.
Only then, can man become righteous and live as Truth.

A Divine Being Just Lives

In the east, the sun has risen,
and the mountains, streams and fields have woken, and are dancing.
There is a cottage nestled in them,
where a child who has woken is chasing baby chicks with a stick,
shadowed by a puppy trotting behind him.
Frogs are leaping around by the stream,
and shoots that had been underground,
are pushing through the earth
and changing from a pale yellow to a vibrant green.
The rowdy people in the lower village
are busily getting ready to farm,
while the frail grannies and grandpas are making porridge.
The womenfolk are in the kitchen,
cooking on a fire stoked with wood and twigs.
The fields are dotted with the menfolk working,
and when the women arrive laden with food,
they eat leisurely in the fields.
Larks are singing in the sky,

and flowers are blossoming in every house in the village.
In the mountains and fields, wild azaleas are in full bloom.
Even though man lives in nature,
his mind puts nature inside him
and he lives his life with greed.
His minds of envy and jealousy form
in his efforts to live a better life than other people,
and to succeed over other people;
he makes the world unclean.
A divine being who has become one with nature
may outwardly lead a life that looks the same as anyone else,
but he does not live in the human world.
He lives in the world of divine beings without any worries;
he lives a life filled with song, sung leisurely.
He lives waiting for the world of divine beings to come;
he lives to make such a world happen.
Even though all people live together,
a divine being lives in heaven,
while man lives inside his own mind.
Therefore, man suffers inside the burden
speaking the words of a ghost.
Only divine beings know the ways of the world,
and live freely, silently and without anxiety.
I was living in the ghost world,
but suddenly arrived in the world of divine beings.

I have become a companion of nature,
a companion of the sky and moon;
I have become the origin that just exists,
and therefore I live a life of freedom;
I just live without greed in the true world,
the complete world, where everything has been cast off.
I live, I just live, without conflict, silently,
like the wind that blows, and water that flows.
I live with the mind of a bird that leisurely sings,
the mind of a deer frolicking in the woods.
It is a mind without thorns;
a mind that is always at rest,
a mind without any greed
because it has let go of everything.
Dead people cannot speak,
but a living person does not speak either.
A divine being just pities sentient beings
who struggle in the *saha* world with burden and suffering.

The Reason And Purpose All Creations Were Born Is To Become Reborn As The Body And Mind Of This Existence And Live Forever

The clear blue sky has not changed;

in the past and now, it just exists.

There is nowhere that this blue sky does not exist -

it exists on Earth where man lives, and in all creations.

This sky before the sky is the origin.

It existed an eternity before, and it will exist an eternity after.

Only the sky remains when the day breaks,

and likewise, if heaven and earth do not exist,

only the original consciousness of the sky exists.

This consciousness is not material;

it is the *Jung* and *Shin* - the body and mind -

that existed before material creation, of and by itself.

It is an existence of oneness, but it consists of *Jung* and *Shin* -

that is, God exists amidst the Emptiness.

The Emptiness is the mother of heaven and earth,

and God - the mind - is the consciousness of all creations.

Everything created in heaven and earth came from this existence.

It is an omnipotent and omniscient entity -

it is God and Buddha - that existed before and after the beginning,
of and by itself.
It is the living existence of Truth;
the existence that is real and alive.
It is complete of and by itself, so its energy is completely real.
It does not lack for anything because Energy and God are one.
A person whose illusionary human body and mind has been resurrected into the body and mind of this existence -
into true Energy and God - does not die.
He will live as an immortal in this land.
This land is energy itself so it exists of and by itself.
The reason and purpose all things were born,
is to be reborn as the body and mind of this existence
and live forever.

The Complete Land

There is nothing; nothing.
There is absolutely nothing,
but amidst the Nothingness, there is Consciousness -
the origin of the creations of heaven and earth;
the master of heaven and earth;
the Creator.
This existence does not exist in man's mind,
so man does not know the Creator.
He must be reborn from the Creator
in order for the world to transform into complete Truth,
and for light to come into the world.
Although absolute nothingness is the origin,
all existences with form are one with it.
The world is already enlightened,
because I am complete.
Since my false self has died, then died again,
only the Lord, who is Truth, remains.
I am reborn with the Lord's body and mind,

and I am in the complete land without death.
The reason man lives -
why his physical form had to appear in the world -
is to be born in the complete land
because his material body can only exist for a limited time.
What exists exists, because existence exists.
We are born in the world through our karmic ties,
we live in the world through our karmic ties,
and we pass away after living in the world through our karmic ties.
When a person has been born in the true world
his Soul and Spirit will live forever.

Untitled 1

The sounds of birds, the wind and water -
the sounds of nature - give my body and mind rest,
but man's world is foul.
People living in the world find life a struggle,
but they do not know the reason behind their hardships
because they are all living inside their own minds.
A person with nowhere to go is always busy,
uselessly and endlessly busy,
no matter how far he goes and goes and goes.
He goes where his countless desires for achievement lead him,
but no matter how far he follows them, there is no final destination.
My heart is full of pity,
because he does not know that the true world
is where he must truly go.

Untitled 2

Man,
insists his world is right.
He does not know it is wrong.
He does not know his greed -
his desires for achievement -
are what burden him.
The reason I am sad
is man is so completely ignorant,
he has become the disciples of past saints,
and believes they are the only saints.
The place he must go is Truth,
and what he must become is Truth.
It is in that place, he gains life from Truth.
He lives and believes blindly,
not knowing there is no Truth, no substance,
in what he believes.
He is truly ignorant beyond ignorance.
I was the same

when I lived with people in the past,
when I was a person of the past.
All things without substance are false.
We must find that which has substance,
and become Truth.

Heaven, Which Is Truth

Heaven, which is Truth,
is freedom,
liberation,
and endless peace,
because in heaven there is no self.
The various things in human life -
good and bad, interesting and boring,
judgment and discrimination,
right and wrong, hot and cold,
suffering and happiness -
do not exist there.
Aging, sickness, birth and death do not exist there;
it is just freedom and liberation.
There, one's mind is the mind of the emptiness itself,
and one just lives.
His mind is the mind of Truth itself -
the eternal and never-changing heaven.
His self of the past is a picture and a very illusion.

In heaven, everything from human life is gone,
and there is nothing but Truth.
In heaven, one has as much happiness and joy
as the blessings he has amassed.
It is paradise.
This land of existence is the real land - the world of reality.
The land that has been resurrected as Truth has no death,
and one lives as an eternal immortal.
A person born in this world is true;
he is Truth;
he is existence;
he does not die;
he lives forever.

The world is complete
but the human mind does not exist,
because in the world of his mind, man takes pictures of the world
like the footage of a video.
The mind of Truth - of God and the origin -
is the true nature that is metaphysical;
it is existence;
time and space do not exist in it;
and it exists of and by itself.
It exists everywhere and within all things;
it existed from the beginning and before the beginning,

and it is the immortal that will exist for an eternity after.
It is the Creator -
this existence itself is the great Soul and Spirit;
it is the source of the infinite Universe, the origin itself;
it is the mother and father of all creation.
When this existence comes to the world as a person,
man and everything in heaven and earth can be saved,
which is the reason it is called the Savior and *Maitreya*.
Having been born in the world,
the only thing that man really needs to do
is to truly live -
he needs to become this existence of Truth.
Only when everything has died
can all creations be resurrected as Truth and live,
for only then can they be reborn.
The land of Truth is the land that is alive,
which man cannot see or know
because he does not have the mind of Truth.
Human completion means to become Truth,
and when man becomes Truth, he can live eternally.
Truth is the place we must get to;
it is the place where we must be reborn;
the place where we must live.
Casting everything off means
one departs from all human matters -

money, love, fame, family and your illusionary self -
for only then can you go to the land of Truth
and be reborn as Truth.
Truth itself must come to the world
in order for man to become Truth and complete.
Man's mind only contains the minds of pictures taken of the world;
it does not have any Truth within it.
Therefore the existence of Truth must come as a person of the world,
and give new birth to man and all creations of heaven and earth.
This is heaven and it is salvation.
Only Truth can take us to the land of Truth
and give us new birth as Truth.
Heaven is the place that exists after the complete death of your false self.
While you are living you must be reborn;
reborn with the body and mind of Truth and completion
and live in the complete land.
Only those who have gone to this land while they are alive
can live in heaven.
It is illogical to believe that you can go to heaven after death
if you are not real and true now.
What is false does not exist -
it will die, it will completely disappear,
because it is an illusion.
Heaven is a place where only those that are true and real live;

it is a place of completion, far from human matters;
A place of freedom and liberation because it is endlessly peaceful;
a place where there is no time and space or any delusions;
a place where one's mind is always at rest
and there is only endless peace.

Haewonsangsaeng - Living In Harmony Free From Bitterness And Regrets

Youth, passed by in vain.
Prime years, passed by in vain.
I am aging along with the years that vanished
in a futile life spent trying to achieve something,
but I have yet to actually do or achieve anything for the world.
The world is a kaleidoscope, a soap-opera.
While living out their various lives
people are busy inside their soap-operas
but they are unable to do what they really must do.
There are many sorrowful events within time that flows by,
but those sorrows do not exist for a person
who does not dwell in what he is trying to achieve -
a person who does not have the mind of sorrows.
But this can only be known
when one does not have the mind of regrets and sorrows.
People live busy, eventful lives
but they are all trapped in their minds,
each creating his own soap-opera.

Human life is futile;
it is a life of a floating weed;
a life of a bubble;
a life of an illusion;
a life inside a dream,
but only a person who has come out from his soap-opera knows this.
The world always just exists,
and only man's dreaming mind constantly changes.
Was there any actual achievements or failures
in a life full of delusional thoughts?
Only one who was woken knows life is dream;
that it is a picture, false, and non-existent.
While living a life of limited time,
one may have heard the vague but certainly spoken words of past saints -
that the poor in spirit are blessed, and heaven theirs,
that man must cleanse and empty his mind.
But these words are useless,
if he does not know how to empty and cleanse his mind.
Yet, there is meaning in human life
for when one cleanses his useless, false mind
and is reborn as the eternal, never-dying mind of God that is real,
he is complete.
Do not blame the world, or the people around you,
and do not let your failed achievements remain as regrets.

Although everything is false,
only he who has discarded the falseness knows that it is so,
and a person who holds onto it, does not know.

The Universe itself is one,
and there is no coming or going,
and because it is one,
only he who has been reborn as the Soul and Spirit,
from the body and mind of the Universe,
can know he lives forever.

Man may look towards heaven and paradise
with the head of a serpent,
but while he is living in his soap-opera,
he cannot be born in this world of one without truly repenting,
and he will wander in his soap-opera for eternity.
That which is real exists;
that which is real is living;
that which is real is the everlasting never-dying existence.
When one becomes reborn as that existence
he will become free from his grudges and regrets
and live happily with others.
Mankind can all live forever,
if all people come to Maum Meditation,
stop blaming others

and get rid of their false illusionary minds
and their selves living inside their minds.
Then this place, here, is heaven and paradise.

Oh, you bubble-like existence!
You do not have a destination
no matter how busily you strive -
do you know where you must go?
A bubble disappears when it bursts,
but only one who has become Truth knows this principle.
Man lives with his evil human mind,
and it is this evil self that strives to achieve Truth,
and desires to become Truth,
but in the end, he is still his evil self.
Truth emerges
when he discards himself completely.
When he is reborn as Truth in the land of Truth,
he will know all the ways of the world;
he will know the Earth, sun and stars in the night sky
that just exists are one;
he will know the rustling wind and flowing river
live according to nature's flow
he will know all things live lives of the original mind -
the mind of nature.

Where are you going, that you go so busily?
You are following a delusion that has nowhere to go
no matter how far it goes and goes.
Where your false self must go,
is the place that is real -
this is where you must truly go.
Don't ask why you are the way you are,
and blame your lot in life.
This mind exists because of the regrets and sorrows
which come from your mind, of what you were unable to have.
So, get rid of your false self and become Truth,
for then, you will lack nothing.

What is true is the way, the life and Truth.
Liberation, which we have only heard of,
is possible only when one's self does not exist.
It is the same for great freedom.
Life in this false world is not real, it is false;
but one can know this only when his self does not exist,
and he has become real.
Only when one's self does not exist,
can he know heaven.
There is a saying that one can know the afterworld only after he is dead,
which means he must die in order to know the ways of the world.

If one becomes the mind of silent nature,
he will be able to live as long as nature lives.

Let go of all your delusional minds -
leave everything to the world,
because the world is the master.
Doesn't everything in nature live born in the world?
There is nothing that is achieved by worrying or being anxious;
this accomplishes nothing.
Take after the world and live with the mind of the world.
The mind of the world is the source, the origin, and the original nature.
It is true, and real, and Truth.
It is the Creator, God, Buddha, and Allah.
It is the origin that everything must return to.
He who holds onto his own mind
is a person who betrays the world, the master.
He will die an eternal death;
he does not exist for he is not real.
A person who has been born as the body and mind of the world and Truth
will live as long as the age of the world.

A Poem Of The World

There is day, and there is night,
there are mountains and there are oceans,
and in the ocean, there are thousands of different life forms.
I had countless different delusional thoughts.
I followed and chased those delusions during the day
and at night, I was lost within them.
I lived inside my mind - the source of all useless thoughts -
and bound inside it, I could not see the world
just as it is, just as one sees it.
I did not know the river tried to persuade my deranged mind
by leisurely flowing past without words,
nor did I know when the wind blew to comfort it.
A demented person does not know what it is that man must do;
I was tied to my mind, I was blind and deaf
to the ways in which the world tried to let me know.
My delusional self only understood words of delusion,
and it was a delusion that believed it was alive or dead.
I wasted all the countless futile years that went by.

Although I wandered and wandered inside my non-existent mind,
I had no destination.
Only later, I realized I had lived inside my mind.
The mind that I had made was one of pictures;
pictures of the world and pictures of my whole life lived in the world.
I had stored them within me and I had lived according to its script.
They were not real; hence, they are pictures.
I had turned my back against the world that is God,
and made my own world, which is sin and karma.
When I escaped from it and became the mind of Truth,
I could see the world is alive;
that the world is already enlightened;
that the world is complete.
Only I had been trapped inside myself and unable to see the world,
because my mind had not been one with the world.
Now that I am reborn in the world,
everything in heaven and earth exist because I exist,
and right here, is heaven.
I have begun to be able to see the trees that are lushly green after rainfall,
and the wild flowers in the fields, whose names I do not know,
that bloom red and blue and yellow.
There is nowhere in the world that is more beautiful than nature,
than this heaven and earth, that God created.

In the past, I could not see anything because I was inside the drama
series of my making.
Everything is created by the providence of nature,
and *this* exists because *that* exists,
and everything that is born, is born into the world
and are therefore the children of the world.
They will live to the age of the world.

The Illusionary Affairs of Human Life

Countless stories in the passage of time have all disappeared.

Man lives with sin and karma because he lives inside his mind.

All things, whether they be good or bad, are pipe dreams and illusions,

and man lives without meaning or purpose within them.

A person who holds onto the affairs of human life

lives with many regrets and sorrows.

He does not know what existence is,

nor does he know non-existence,

and he lives bound to the futile matters of human life.

Only silent nature and the silent world

know man's foolishness.

Man does not know why he lives,

and he lives ignorant of where he must go,

which is the place where he can become Truth,

and that this is to achieve everything.

In order to be reborn as Truth, one's illusionary self must not exist;

only when it does not exist can one have the viewpoint of Truth.

This is something only a person who has become Truth knows,
and only he can put this knowledge into action.
Only a person who has been to heaven can know heaven.
The many stories which have gone with the years
only exist because man holds onto them.
But a person whose mind is heaven itself does not contain stories;
he lives adjusting to reality, just as it is.
The future only exists for a person who has a mind of past stories,
and he has worries because of this mind.
But he whose mind has become real
does not have the human mind world
so he is free and liberated,
and he lives free from all affairs of human life.
He who has the non-existent human mind is dead within it,
and he lives with suffering and burden inside a non-existent world.
The world is already complete,
and the world is already enlightened,
but only man is not one with the world
and is dead inside himself.
The master of heaven and earth must come
for heaven and earth to be able to live.
What is real must come to heaven and earth,
for man to become real.
Only he who has become real can know
everything man desires to achieve has no meaning.

What is real is the origin -

the source that existed before the world -

and the world.

Man believes he is living in the world

but he does not live in the world -

he lives in his mind that is overlapping the world.

The only salvation is for falseness to become real,

and such a person will be reborn and live in the real world -

the eternally indestructible Truth.

The Life Truth Leads When It Is Born In The World

Past saints spoke of the affairs of life being futile, in vain, and like a bubble,
because human life is limited in time.
I teach man about the futility, vanity and bubble-like qualities of life so that he can become real,
after which I teach him it is not futile, or in vain or bubble-like after all.
I teach him about the place of the origin -
the place before great nature came forth.
I make him return to the origin completely,
so that he can be reborn there as Truth.
Man lives immaturely.
His self is a dream and the problem is he holds onto his self
and wishes for his false self to be able to live.
I can only sigh, without saying anything,
pitying the poor sentient beings.
One's illusionary self lives without knowing
where it must go or even whether it is alive

because he lives unaware that he is false.
What exists in the world is real
but man is non-existent because he is not in the world.
He is non-existent because he does not live in the world.
What is in the world exists,
but what is not in the world does not.
Man does not know this
because he has never become the perspective of the world.
All scriptures were written from the world's perspective,
and the origin of Truth must come to the world as a person
if man is to become Truth.
A person who teaches Truth must be the existence of Truth
if his teachings enable people to actually become Truth.
People want to become Truth themselves,
but they are unwilling to accept that the person teaching them
is also Truth.
Man does not become Truth because of anything he himself does;
it is done for him by Truth.
Man believes he lives in the world because of his own greatness,
but he is an illusion that only cares about himself.
What is complete in the world,
what has been born in the land of *Jung* and *Shin*,
just exists, no matter how much you destroy or get rid of it.
What disappears when it is destroyed or eliminated is an illusion,
and it has not been born in the world.

When non-existence exists,

it is because it has been born in the real world;

for such is what exists and what lives.

The world is heaven and paradise,

and he who is born as such lives a life of Truth.

The Mountains, Streams And Nature Are Alive

The mountains and streams are blue and green,
and crystal clear water flows in the ravine.
In the gorge, a squirrel scurries away scared,
while a pheasant flies away.
There is an unidentifiable bird flying in the sky
and azaleas, rhododendrons and white flowers
bloom in the trees.
Silver-vine leaves are growing on silver-vine trees
and wild aster leaves can also be seen.
We are following a path made for putting out mountain-fires,
on our way to forage for mountain herbs.
From inside the mini-van, the mountain scenery is spectacular.
The path is just wide enough to accommodate the van,
and we follow the meandering road until we reach the peak.
The mountain at springtime is too beautiful
for it to be seen only by the few people who are here.
Stained through by their lives in the cities,
people here mingle with nature,

and as they forage for herbs without any human minds,
they become brighter as their toxic human minds disappear.
The ravine is too steep to climb,
but I would like to travel up the water course.
There is a decrepit shack
and it is impossible to know who lived there
and why it is now so disheveled.
I think awhile about why someone might have lived here.
The spring air is neither hot nor cold,
and makes me want to prolong this moment for as long as possible.
Further down, there are villages are nestled in every valley,
and stories of their long inhabitance have been passed down through
    the ages.
They were settled by fugitives from the Korean-Japanese war of the
    1500's,
who escaped deep into these mountains,
so deep it is still inaccessible by car.
I'm told most people have now moved out into the cities.
The water flowing valley after valley is so clear,
and the rocks and pebbles carved by the flowing water through the
    years are pristinely clean,
showcasing the beauty of the hills behind Mt. Gaya,
where divine beings supposedly lived.
One must cleanse his mind in order to be a divine being,
and only he who has cleansed his mind can know

man must repent his evil mind of sin and karma.
There are many stories of people all over the world,
but people of the past exist because their descendants currently exist;
those who have gone are silent, and they do not exist in the world.
They are all futile affairs of human life.
No matter how much time passes,
it is possible to just live, outside of time,
if man is born in the world.
Then man would still be alive,
but his soul is not able to live as long as the age of the world
because he is not born in the world.
I drink a bowl of *makgeolli* in a tavern
and alone I ponder on the following matters:
a divine being who created other divine beings has never existed in the world;
a Buddha who made other Buddhas has never existed;
there has never been saints or schools who have made more saints.
Màn struggles and strives to live man's false lifetime,
but a wise person discards himself in order to live to the age of the world -
a lifetime of the world.
This is something that is truly commendable,
it is something to be thankful for.
Man's life is futile, but a person born as Truth

lives forever in the true world.

This is why man was born as a human-being,

this is what man was born to do,

and this is where he must go - where he must live.

However, he does not know this because he is a man.

He simply keeps living his illusionary life,

and feeling sorry for man,

I order another bowl and drink.

He Who Is Born In Heaven Lives In Heaven While He Who Is Born On Earth Lives On Earth

From man's point of view,
the sky is at times cloudy, at times empty,
and sometimes it is blue.
It is seen in many different ways,
but the true sky is the living Holy Spirit and Holy Ghost,
namely, it is the great Soul and Spirit itself.
The place of absolute emptiness is the place of the Holy Spirit,
and where the one God exists amidst the emptiness
is the place of the Holy Ghost.
The word *holy* is affixed because this existence is alive,
and creates heaven, earth and all creations.
Man is born on earth,
and he has the earth he has copied from the world in his mind.
He who is born on earth lives on earth
because man lives inside this mind.
He who is born in heaven - the sky -
is he who has been reborn as the holy Soul and Spirit of Truth.
This means he will do the work of heaven and live in heaven.

He is one who does not have a false and illusionary self at all.

Only when the master of this land has come as a person,

can man be born in heaven,

can man become Truth,

and can man be born and live in that land.

He Who Has Become A Proper Person Will Teach Properly And Live Properly

The world is already enlightened,
and the world is one of light, as bright as day.
However, man cannot see this bright world
because his consciousness is trapped inside his mind world.
People who are ignorant of the world of light
live in suffering because they do not know what true light is.
They live inside their dark minds according to what is scripted there;
they live within their sufferings and their burdens,
oblivious of where they must go.
Man blames life and the events of life,
but he does not know he is the one to blame.
Man, who lives inside his mind, within endless time,
does not know his mind itself is an illusion and a ghost.

All people, whether they be kind or unsatisfied,
whether they be family, friends, or enemies
are illusions and ghosts from the viewpoint of the world of light.

They are all illusions and entities that do not exist.
People have not been able to live how they wish -
according to their wills that are their greed -
and they have many regrets and sorrows
because they live with non-existent entities,
speak with non-existent entities,
and live out their various lives with non-existent entities.
Although much time has passed, and is still passing by,
this problem cannot and will not be solved from within man's mind.
There will come a day when man becomes righteous and stands tall,
a time when everyone lives in the land of light,
and only then will this problem of man be solved.
Moreover, the resolution of all suspicions and doubts will happen
when man knows they arise from his delusions,
and that these delusions, and his self, are false.
Only when one comes out into the light that is Truth,
does he know life is an illusion
and that it happens inside a dream.
Only he who has been born in the world of light has wisdom,
and does not live foolishly;
and therefore does not have darkness within him.
Great nature that is silent lives in the land of light without anxieties,
but it is deeply unfortunate that man who speaks too much
is dead, trapped in the world of darkness.

Man being reborn as Truth and as a complete person,
and living an eternal life as an immortal,
is something we have only heard and read in scriptures,
but it is truly happening - it is becoming fulfilled.
It is difficult to know whether this is a dream or reality.
A miracle is falseness becoming Truth,
and that which is non-existent becoming existent,
so is it not a miracle of miracles,
that the whole world is being created to become truly existent?
Religions wait for a Savior, *Maitreya* or *Jung-do-ryung*,
but these refer to the existence of Truth,
and man does not know Truth.
He must become Truth in order to know the Savior, *Maitreya*, and *Jung-do-ryung*.
Making man who is false become real is salvation
and such is the work of the Savior.
The world is alive,
but this world can only be saved and changed into a true and real world by the Savior,
and only Truth can make man become Truth.
Even at this moment, there are people all over the world trying to become Truth,
by searching here and there and trying all kinds of things,
but man can become Truth,
only when his body and mind are resurrected as the world that is

Truth.
The countless trials and tribulations,
the events and stories of the world
happen within the mind man made;
there are no worries in the land of light that is Truth
and one just lives with the mind of nature.
Laying down the affairs of life that do not exist,
and escaping from one's conceptions and habits,
so that one can live in the world that is true,
is what all people must urgently do.
This is the only way to receive salvation
and the only way to be born and live in the world with wisdom.
It is then that mankind can become one
and everyone can live with laughter.
If the people of the world cleanse their minds and are born as Truth,
there will be never-ending laughter because they are Truth,
and everyone can live happily.
It is for one's own sake, in order to live a good life, that wars arise,
and it is for one's own prosperity and success that he preys on others.
However when one does not have any human minds,
he will live for other people.
Government and politics should be run by those who have done Maum Meditation,
as religions, philosophy, ideology and learning should also be,

for they will be done and led in the right way
only when they are taken over by those who have cleansed their minds
and become Truth.
Only he who has discarded all and has been resurrected as Truth is a proper person,
and only such a person knows the way to live as Truth.
Truth and falseness may seem as though they are the same,
but there is a world of difference
from one whose consciousness is trapped inside himself
to one who has become the consciousness of the world -
it is the difference between heaven and earth.

One's Life After He Has Become Real

None of the events and stories I had in my mind exists in the world;
they are all illusions I made.
I had stored everything in my mind,
and I had lived within it,
but now, that world and I do not exist,
and the real world - the source - that is existence and the origin remains.
I am born from the origin,
and my Soul and Spirit is the incarnation of the origin.
Because I do not exist, it is freedom;
and because I do not exist, it is liberation and great rest.
The Creator created the world and he also created man.
The Creator must come to the world in human form,
for all people to be resurrected as the Creator's children
in the land of the Creator and for man and the world to be born in the real world.
Isn't it a miracle of miracles that this can happen?
That man can become complete and live forever is a true miracle,

but because man who is false does not know Truth,
he does not know what to believe and what is actually true.
Shouldn't we be thankful to the origin,
and acknowledge this inconceivable grace -
this debt of having become Truth,
by becoming of one mind with the will of the origin,
and dedicate our whole lives to saving world and its people
by helping them to be resurrected and make this world a heaven and paradise?

Now that I have discarded everything and I do not exist,
the world is the living heaven, and this itself is eternal blessing and happiness.
My mind that had nowhere to go no matter where I went,
my mind that only sought to gain,
now that it has become Truth and gained everything,
it does not lack anything,
and all delusional thoughts have completely disappeared,
and the five desires and seven sins no longer exist.

I am so thankful; there is only thankfulness,
because none of this was achieved by me,
it was all done for me by Truth.
Just as it was done unconditionally and without expectations of anything in return,

I will live saving the world,
also without the mind that I do so.

Casting off the meaningless affairs of human life,
and amassing blessings in the land of Truth,
is what a wise person, a person of Truth, does.

It is in heaven that you must have power,
by amassing your blessings in that everlasting land.
This is what it means when it is said,
that the wise store their treasures in heaven,
while fools store their treasures on earth.

Because I do not exist, it is great freedom,
and the world is the land without death,
where one knows all the ways of the world.
Only a person who lives in that land,
knows man's importance and worth,
and the meaning of life.
Man who is at the crossroads of life and death should not hesitate;
he should be born in the world that is true.
Looking back from that world,
the affairs of human life were all foolish,
and now that my false self, the ghost, has gone,
there are no regrets at all.

It was truly difficult to get rid of myself,

and it is amazing and a relief that I have disappeared.

I do not even want to look back.

My regrets and sighs have fled, and all suffering and burdens have gone.

I had tried to gain Truth holding onto myself,

but now that I have gone, I have become Truth

and my Soul and Spirit of Truth is now truly reborn.

Like the bird that flies in the sky,

like all things that exist in the world,

I can just live, I can lay down all minds.

I live having become the mind of nature.

It is so wonderful,

that I will dedicate my whole body

and the rest of my lifetime,

to helping people to come to this world.

The Best Way To Do Maum Meditation

Recognize that you are an illusion,
and that you deserve to die for being an illusion and a ghost.
Even if you do not have the things that exist within the seven levels
of the meditation method,
recognize that you do not deserve to have them:
a ghost does not deserve to have money, love, fame, family,
pride, enemies or the ghost world.

The most difficult task in the world,
is to make man become Truth,
and those who are not able to become Truth
even when they have a method to do so, will die
because they are foolish.

The Savior, Maitreya, And *Jung-do-ryung* Is The Person Who Creates Things That Are Real

If my mind had not existed,
I would have lived with a mind that reached the world -
I would have lived with the mind of the world.
But because of my mind, I could not become the world,
and I did not exist in the world.

Everyone lives out their life inside his mind of pictures,
and waits for the Savior to come.
Only a Savior who can make falseness become Truth, can give salvation.
Such a person is Truth itself, or in other words,
the person who has come in human form as Truth itself is the Savior.
The *Jung-do-ryung* is the person who teaches the definition of *dō*,
who teaches the proper *dō*, and makes people become *dō* itself.
Maitreya is the person who makes people become one with the mind of the world,
and makes this world a paradise.

The Savior is the person who makes people become Truth while they are living,
and takes them to heaven, where only people of Truth live.

Such a person will have a solution, a way, to make people become Truth.
If there is a place where one can be born as Truth by cleansing his human mind,
the solution, the way, will be there.
Man does not know the place where Truth can be found,
because he does not know what Truth is.
The book of prophecy, *Kyuk-am-yu-rok*,
told us to go to the place where one can cleanse his mind,
and it also told us to go to the place where the cow lows.
This means that we must go to the place
where we can become enlightened by cleansing our minds.
When one's self no longer exists, the place of Truth appears.
He will then become this existence itself,
which is the completion of man.
Human completion is when man who is false becomes real and Truth.

The Age Of Man I

When I told people to go to heaven,
a person approached me and asked where heaven is.
When I told him that it is inside man's mind,
he did not think much of my answer.
Heaven - the land of existence - is the world that man receives
when his mind, the world that takes self-centered pictures, disappears
and he becomes the complete mind of God.
Man becomes complete, when he has become the mind of God,
and it is in the land of that mind,
the master of the true consciousness allows him to live again.
This is what it is to be reborn with true consciousness.
The master of heaven and earth created all material things,
and when the master of heaven and earth comes as a person,
man can be reborn and live in the land of true consciousness.
All creations can live in this land of true consciousness,
by this master's will.

They are resurrected and they live by the words of the world's master.

Only the master of the world who is a human-being can give salvation.

The Mind Of The Origin

The river flows, and is going somewhere,
and my heavy mind wants to follow it and leave.
The river flows silently, always downward from a high place,
according to the universal order of nature.
On the other hand, man's delusional thoughts flit back and forth
but he has not actually achieved anything in the world.
The waves rise when the wind blows
and they are joined by the rain when it falls.
The water gives life to countless plants and vegetation,
and although it does many things, it is silent;
It does not even have the thought that it does what it does.
It just lives, having become the origin,
having become the mind of nature itself.
A person who has gone to the origin,
is able to lay everything down and just live.
He is able to do so because he does not have a self,
and he is free of everything from the material world.
He who has gone to the origin,

has departed from all human thoughts and agonies,
and he who has gone to the origin,
has transcended all sorts of things from the material world
and is a complete person.
The origin is a place where only a person whose body and mind
have completely disappeared can go,
but even so, the master of the origin must give birth to him in that
land -
that is, he can only live when he is saved by the master;
he can live there only when the master allows him to do so.
What is real and eternally alive is Truth;
it is the origin, one's original nature,
the source, the genesis,
God, Buddha,
Haneol-nim, Allah and one;
but at the same time this existence itself is *Jung* and *Shin*,
the Holy Spirit and the Holy Ghost,
the Holy Spirit and the Holy Father,
Dharmakaya and *Sambhogakaya.*
They refer to the body and mind of the origin,
but are expressed differently.
All creations were born according to their conditions,
by receiving the body and mind of this existence itself.
This existence is the Creator,
and it is omnipotent and omniscient.

Omnipotence is the ability to create all of creation,
and because it does so, it is omnipotent.
It is omniscient, because being God and the source of the Universe,
it knows all principles of the Universe.

The mind of God is a mind that has departed from everything;
it is complete, so although it is living,
it is a mind that has no thought - no mind - that it is alive.
It is a complete place, free from human minds
that discerns this is this, and that is that.
It is a mind of non-existence, the mind of the emptiness.
Although God is alive,
the reason it does not have even the mind of being so,
is it has transcended life, and lives a true life
that is free from all human conceptions and habits.
It is great freedom, and liberation itself,
but it exists in the real world and it is alive.
He who has become like this
can live like the wind and water
because he has become Truth.

We Must Come Out From The Shadows, The Illusions, Into The World

Man has the mind of shadows,
and he lives in a shadow of the world.
Man thinks he is living in the world,
but he is not, because he takes pictures of the world
and on the stage of that mind of pictures,
he lives according to what is scripted in this mind,
as a slave to it.
Since he lives with this mind,
he is just an extra in a tragic play on that stage.
In this mind, there are all sorts of things:
there is this and that, judgment and discrimination,
aging, sickness, life and death,
the five desires and seven sins;
there is coming and going, cold and hot,
high and low, the great and the inferior.
It is a particularly difficult life,
because he is staging his opera on a fake stage.
Man thinks that he lives in the world because he is great,

but the world comes first, and he should be ashamed
for stealing everything in the world after being born in that world.
He should have just lived, as he was made and placed in the world -
what need was there to steal what belongs to the world
to make his own picture world?
This has only ever increased man's suffering and burden
and stopped him from living with freedom.

Your stage is not real but fake and a picture.
If you think about the fact that you are living in a picture,
isn't it clear that it is terrible and without life;
that it is illusionary?
If you escape from the illusionary stage,
and come out and live in the world of Truth,
you will have no worries,
and you will have the freedom of freedoms.
Such a life sets everyone and everything in the world free.
All human thoughts are pictures and illusions,
and they are all useless.
They are all futile delusions,
and even the fact that you are living is a delusion,
so you must come out from your mind world,
in order for you to live.

The Land Of God Where Time Does Not Exist

The countless memories that disappeared with time
remain in my heart.
Time flowed by silently; no, there was no flowing by at all,
but my memories remain in my heart
and there are times when I miss those years, those times,
and at other times, I despise and blame them.
Sometimes they give me joy,
and sometimes, I don't even want to think about them.
Time does not speak,
and silent time does not go anywhere, but just exists -
only my mind comes and goes.

Everyone lives with useless dreams that have already passed,
and it is because of them, that their minds exist.
Just living, or just living in the world
is a life lived not with that mind, but with the mind of Truth.
The mind of time that comes and passes - the man-made mind -
is a mind that is limited to the length of human life,

but the mind that has surpassed this state,
does not have the mind of coming or going,
and time does not exist within it.
If one becomes free from the useless delusional human mind,
and is reborn as Truth, his delusional self no longer exists;
he is reborn as God that is Truth.
Therefore, his self of the past that lived in the past disappears somewhere,
and only God that is now himself remains.
The world that disappears with time,
is the world of ghosts.

All the events in my life were of the ghost world.
Only nature that is silent lives in the world of God,
adjusting to everything in nature.
It is able to do so, because it has the mind of nature.
When I look back, everyone who lived a human lifetime
lived a life of a bubble,
and their human lifetimes were everything they had.
They have all disappeared.
He who is free from time, lives without time,
in the complete world where time does not exist.
I teach people how to become free from time,
and I teach how to live a lifetime of the world.
When one's mind becomes the real world,

a person of the real world is born.
From the beginning, the true world is myself,
and the master of the true world is myself,
so birth in the true world is also done by me.
Without going through me,
no one can go to heaven that is the true world.
If man is to go to the true world,
the prerequisite is to become Truth.
The world is a place where one lives without time,
and because time does not exist, naturally there is no death,
and the land of God is eternal and invincible.
Only he who has been liberated from time
will live free from time.

A Life Lived By Truth

When a storm blows,
all creations hold their breath,
and submit to the might of the storm.
When the storm passes after raging awhile,
everything is simply as it was;
as if there had never been a storm.
It is the same with human affairs:
if there are dark and cloudy days,
there are also days that are clear.
Namely, time solves everything.
While taking man to the peak of completion,
incomplete people had much to say
and incomplete people spoke and behaved how they wanted,
but even in the thick of that storm,
I was dragging them to the peak.
At the peak where the storm does not blow,
it is infinitely peaceful and quiet.
Looking back from the peak,

I think people had trouble following me here
because they lacked dedication and diligence.
Human completion is discarding one's false body and mind,
and being reborn with the body and mind of the origin that is real.
Those whose sly and cunning minds wanted to become complete,
those who sought Truth in order to become superior,
all ended up dying.
The clean and sublime place of Truth,
cannot be achieved while holding onto one's self;
it is achieved by completely discarding all of one's self.
When there is no self, only that which is real remains,
and one can only be born if Truth
enables him to be born in the world of Truth.
If one is resurrected as what is real in the land that is real,
his self, the person of the past that is false, dies
and his real self is born in the real land.
He can become real in the land that is real
by the words commanding his self that is real to be born.
Such is what Truth is.
What is profound and mysterious is the real world,
which man cannot understand, for he is false.
The land that is real was created by the existence that is real,
by his words, *be reborn*.
Those who meet the requirements can live,
namely, those who do not have a self,

only when the existence that is real
allows them to be born in the real land.
The people of the world live with falseness that is not real,
and they pretend to be clever, and believe that they are clever,
but they do not actually know anything -
everything they know is false.
Man speaks, behaves and lives according to what his mind holds,
and because his mind is not real but falseness itself,
there is nothing he knows.
What he knows is an illusion,
acquired by taking pictures of the world.
It does not exist in the world and it is not real,
so it is the epitome of an illusion.
Within this illusion, it can be said that people's lives progressed,
but it was progress that is not true progress.
And in the end, for their own sakes,
they killed and were killed,
they stole and robbed;
there are many, many people
who lost their humanity and are at odds with the world.
In a self-centered world where one wants to live better
and do better than others, all he gains is loneliness;
and even if he himself succeeds and lives a good life,
his descendants end up failing and suffering.
Man's happiness comes from living without worries,

and the mind of happiness is one that wishes for others to live well.
Man has as much anguish as what he has in his mind,
but he does not have anguish if in his mind there is no greed.
He who has, or holds, in his mind what he possesses,
ends up suffering even more when his possessions disappear
because he has them in his mind.
If there is nothing in one's mind,
he has no worries, whether he possesses something or not.
If man is reborn as the real mind - the mind of great nature -
he will live according to universal order, just as nature does,
because he will not have any human minds.
He will live adapting to the world,
and everyone will live as one.
Everyone will live in togetherness, as "we" rather than "me",
and the world will become *our* world -
a place of one.

Part 5

The master of the original foundation must come as a human-being in order for everything in the world to be eternally saved.

The Age Of Man II

Little bird, little bird, where are you going?
Where did you come from,
and where is it that you are going?
A bird lives flitting from tree to tree silently,
and it passes away while searching for food.
It lives just doing what it needs to do,
and it lives without worrying.
Man has put so many events and stories inside himself,
that even the sound of the bird whistling
causes countless thoughts to arise like bubbles in boiling porridge.
He is lost in his own thoughts
and cannot hear the bird's singing.
But he who can hear the singing of the bird,
knows the wonder and mystery of nature
because his thoughts come from a mind that has become nature;
because his mind is the mind of nature
and can be at leisure and magnanimous.
The flowing river just flows,

and the trees in the mountains just live,
but only man lives with greed in his mind
and is unable to fulfill his purpose.
The true will, or purpose, that man needs to achieve
is to become a person; that is, he needs to become a real person -
a real person has become the mind of nature that is silent and is therefore living,
but he is at the state where he has transcended the fact that he exists;
the state where he has transcended death;
the state that is beyond joy, sadness, good, bad, existence, non-existence,
cold, hot, cool, warm, joy, anger, sorrow and pleasure.
It is the land where one's Soul and Spirit,
the complete existence that has become Truth, lives.
The ordinary person tries to become Truth while holding onto his self,
but a wise person tries to become Truth by throwing away his useless self.
Great nature teaches man about life,
but man cannot see or understand what nature teaches him
because he has not become the mind of great nature.
Inside the mind that he has made,
he does not think of the ways of great nature,
and he lives according to his own will,

and his will is to live only for his own sake.
Without reason or purpose, man ages,
and without reason or purpose, he leaves the world.
He who lives within his mind,
lives trapped inside his mind, a non-existent world,
and without knowing that this is death,
he lives suffering and burdened,
going through the cycle of death and rebirth, over and over again.
He who has completely died and become the mind of nature,
is the Soul and Spirit of the great Universe,
and within nature, he is an eternal immortal.
Such a person has cast off everything;
he is free and liberated,
because he is free from the source of man's suffering -
he is free from human conceptions and habits.
Only a person who has completely died can go to this place,
and he can only be born there, when none of his self exists.

No matter where he goes man has nowhere to go,
because regardless of how much he does and achieves,
they are done in his mind,
and his achievements are non-existent illusions.
The purpose, the reason, man was born into the world,
is to become complete and to become Truth.
Truth is where he must go, and Truth is where he must live.

Weary wanderer, though you may walk and walk, there is no end;
let's go to Truth and have eternal peace.
Let's live eternally.
Do not live a human lifetime that can be seen,
but live a lifetime of the world.
To live a lifetime of the world,
you must be reborn as an eternal and indestructible existence -
the Soul and Spirit, the *Jung* and *Shin*, of the Universe.
Only this existence is alive,
and only this existence is Truth and real.
Man's false body and mind are illusions and therefore useless,
so if you discard it, the Universe which is the origin remains.
You must be resurrected
and receive a new body as the Soul and Spirit of the Universe.
It is the age of man.
It is an age when man is respected,
an age when man becomes the master of the Universe.
The world lives or dies according to man's will,
and only when man, a human-being, is the master of the world that is true,
can the true world be saved within man,
and man saved within the true world.
In this time, this age, of human completion,
we should repent and go to heaven while we are living.
Man's perpetual riddle was how to become complete,

which he could not achieve for thousands,
no, for tens of thousands of years.
But now, the riddle is solved - it can be fulfilled
when everyone stops thinking that only he himself is right
and goes to the place where man can become complete.
Can you believe in a heaven you are told of only with words?
Would you throw away your one and only life?
If not, you must become complete while you are living, immediately,
and you must go to heaven while you are still living, immediately.
If the place where you are practicing or attending is real,
then shouldn't you have become real already?
No matter what form the real existence has when he comes to the world,
if he makes people become real,
then isn't he the real existence?
Don't wait for a Savior with a particular form,
but have an open mind and if there is a method to become real,
take a leap of faith and try it, because you will become real.
Regardless of whether Truth has come or gone,
people are unable to see,
so do not try to see Truth with your eyes.
If there is a place where one can become Truth,
then that place is Truth.
The place of Truth, is where you can become true,

not the place that talks of what is true.

A person who is attached to scriptures will continue to live within the scriptures

even when everyone else has become true.

Just as the Jews were not able to receive Jesus

because they were too bound to the Old Testament,

when it is said that Jesus will come back to the world on a cloud accompanied by angels,

it means man will not know when Truth comes to the world;

when those who have become Truth come to the world in human form.

Man is trapped inside his mind world

and is unable to see the person from heaven.

People, who are limited by their idea of what Truth looks like,

will not know when *Maitreya* comes to the world,

and they will not know when *Jung-do-ryung* comes to the world.

All these terms speak of one existence -

the existence of Truth - coming to the world.

This existence will be the existence that makes Truth.

Spring, Summer, Fall and Winter

On a bright spring day, a heat wave undulates;
a person comes bearing an a-frame on his back
laden with the azaleas he has picked.
The single ladies who have gone to forage for wild edible herbs
pick wild chives and mugwort leaves in a neighboring village field,
and come back bearing huge filled baskets on their heads.
The married women of the village are doing their laundry in a rocky
spring
and thanks to the spring air, all sorts of things are sprouting by the
stream.
When warm spring comes,
men walk in the furrows between the barley fields;
worried that its house built there will come to harm,
a lark cries from up in the sky.
Once in a while, cars pass by on the new unpaved road,
raising up a cloud of dust.
Near the river, there are people digging for clams
while the single men and women catch chickens to cook porridge

and partake in a traditional pastime of looking at flowers
and eating flower pancakes.
There are girls swinging on a tree swing, wearing brightly colored *han-bok* clothing.
The lovely season of spring is called the barley hump,
because during this time there are people who do not have enough to eat;
often they can only fill their bellies with seasoned wild herbs.
When spring passes, and summer arrives,
the trees in the mountains become a lush green,
and the children who should be tending the cows,
leave them to graze in the pastures while they play in the water all day,
their hands and feet becoming swollen and shriveled like prunes.
When from time to time men who have gone abroad come back home,
everyone knows which families they belong to and who they are.
When they return home after the cows are fed, and the hay has been collected,
they eat pumpkin mush and noodles, wolfing it down as fast as they can.
In the fields, the rice shoots that were planted in the spring are growing,
while in another plot, bean and cotton plants are thriving.
In the mountains, there are graves here and there,

and it is easy to find out whose graves they are, from which family.
A man returns from the market that is a few miles away;
he comes back drunk and empty-handed,
having spent all the money that was earmarked for groceries.
It was earned by selling his precious produce,
and his wife's raised voice can be heard, scolding him.
The mosquito smudge drives away the mosquitoes for awhile,
but without it, they come back in droves.
At night, both the young and old gather with their friends to talk,
and the single boys and girls gather together to play.
During the fall, there are sports days and the harvest festival,
and the crops planted in the spring and summer
are gathered bale by bale, then spread out in the field.
The trees that were green in the summer
begin to turn red and orange,
while the grass changes to a faded yellow.
When strong winds begin to blow,
it signals the beginning of winter.
In the winter, people go to collect firewood,
and at night, they sometimes steal *kimchi* to eat,
or even chickens, and play cards under a kerosene lamp.
Late at night, when they are ready to head home,
the floor has cooled and is chilly.
In foreign lands, far, far away,
some places have four seasons - spring, summer, fall and winter.

In some places it is summer all year long,
and there are other places that have only summer and winter,
but no fall or spring.
There are many different kinds of places in the world.
When I was younger, I often went hiking,
and in my own way, thought a lot about the futility of life.
The mountain scenery was always different,
in spring, summer, fall and winter,
no matter how often I went.
Famous mountains gained their fame
for being similar to the haunts of divine beings.
I come from a small country,
and to me, America seems so big and wide.
Here in this place, my will, my purpose, will be fulfilled:
A world without divisions between nations is being made,
and mankind will become one.

Let's Become True People

The wanderer is silent.
The insane have taken land that does not belong to them,
and have split it up amongst themselves,
but the wanderer is silent;
he does not say anything because he is magnanimous.
Believing that they live in the world because of their own greatness,
and living according to their own will,
the insane cannot hear the words of the wanderer.
It is an insane world that only has insane people in it,
and although a person of the true world has come to his own world,
he has nowhere to dwell or rest because they strongly believe that it
is their world.
The world belongs to the wanderer,
but the insane have made it theirs.
The true master has become a wanderer,
and insane ghosts, that are nameless and non-existent in the world,
have gathered and live by their self-made rules and regulations.
What the saints told us of Truth,

insane ghosts have explained and interpreted in their own way,
however they pleased.
Thus one book that has one message,
has tens of thousands of different interpretations,
splitting religions into tens of thousands of different sects and denominations.
Which of the insane ghosts' religions is the right one?
Isn't someone who claims something is right
when it is completely wrong, a person who is insane?
To be right is to be proper,
and to be proper is to be correct,
and to be correct is Truth.
What has not become Truth is not right.
Insane ghosts must treat their insanity,
and become a correct and true person.
An insane ghost who does not know he is insane,
believes he is right and correct,
and the problem is, that is all he knows.
This is because this is how big his "plate"- his mind - is
and that is all it holds.
An insane ghost is an illusion that does not exist in the world,
because he has falseness, not Truth, in his mind,
and he lives within the world of this mind.
He jabbers on about illusions, so he is insane and a ghost.
In the world, what is actually right is a person who lives in the

world,
a person who has been born again with the body and mind of the world.
Such a person is right, proper and correct.
This world itself is completely correct and proper,
but only man is not so.
Man is in a world that does not exist in the world,
a world made by taking pictures of the world.
If man, the insane ghost, knew this, he would weep.
It is possible for the insane ghost to know this,
when he eliminates his self that is the insane ghost,
and he is born as a true person.
If this happens, there will be no wanderers in the world,
and everyone will become masters.
In the world of insane ghosts, in the world where they live,
the true person is regarded as being wrong.
To them, he will be thought of as being a heretic and a cult figure.
But if people truly think that they are right,
they must ask themselves, whether or not they have become Truth.
It may then be possible for them to realize the Truth.

I came to the world, having become the master of the world,
and I have found that all people are insane ghosts.
Treating this mental illness is the most urgent thing to be done.
An insane ghost must be coaxed, soothed, humored and praised,

before it can be asked to discard its insane mind,
because an insane ghost's mind is fickle and changes by the minute.
It is harder than babysitting a child.
Insane ghosts speak and behave according to whatever they have put
inside their minds;
they are all mad, and only the doctor that has come to treat them is
in his right mind,
so it is no easy feat for the doctor to come to their world
and give them new birth with true minds.
Ghosts are only happy when they are praised;
if they are told that someone other than they are right or great,
they do not believe it.
But even in the world of insane ghosts,
the people who longed for stories of the true world are a little easier
to handle,
as are those who have lost the many possessions they had.
When this loss eventually leads them to Truth,
they are overjoyed and count their earlier losses as true blessings.
An insane ghost will die eventually, at some point in time,
leaving behind all he has and everything that belongs to him.

Where must one go and where must one live?
Only he who has become real will know.
All those who live bound to the futile affairs of human life must all
be reborn as real people,

so that we can make this world a paradise, a nation for all people;
a place where our descendants can sleep without worrying;
and a world where everyone can live with joy.
We must build a world where a real person, the master of the world,
can rest,
a world where everyone can live in togetherness.
Only when all people chase out the insane ghosts,
and are born as true people, can this end be achieved.

The True World

Man believes he is right and others are wrong.
He agrees with things that fit his conceptions and habits,
and disagrees when they do not.
All of man's behaviors and words
are self-centered conceptions and habits.
They are not real; they are false pictures.
There is nothing right in any of them.
Only Truth is right;
only what is proper is right;
only what exists is right - only that which is not non-existent,
namely, only that which is in the world is proper and right.
The conceptions and habits of one's mind are not right at all.
What man thinks he knows are all minds, pictures, stored in one's picture world,
thus, nothing is right in the world.
No one's actions are right either,
for they are done or spoken from the picture world.
When a person has not been born in the world,

all of his actions are wrong, because nothing he does is Truth.
To truly know something, one has to become the world;
one only truly knows when he has become the viewpoint of the world.
The perspective of one's self is just his own conceptions;
it is not Truth, so he does not truly know anything.
A person who does not have self, a person who is self-less,
is Truth and such a person speaks true words and behaves truly.
A person who has a self, speaks and behaves from his own point of view,
so there is nothing right in his words or actions.
Man should live not in his illusionary conceptions and habits,
but with the viewpoint of Truth.
If man sees the world properly with clear eyes;
if he listens to what the world is saying with keen ears,
and if he speaks true words and behaves in a true way,
the world will become a bright place.

An Immigrant Must Go To The Place Where He Can Become Truth, Man Must Go To The Place Where He Can Become Truth

The land is as wide as wide can be,
but only a few people live here in the Americas.
It was inhabited by Indians in the past,
but now it is mostly populated by European immigrants
who have settled here.
It is not a densely populated place.
There are birds and creatures here that I do not recognize,
rare mountains and plains that I have never seen,
and many different kinds of tropical fruit.
But life here is not so different from the East -
people here also eat and live.
Having come from a small country,
I am envious of the wide land.
The majority of the Koreans who have immigrated here
have their own businesses, from which they make their living.
In South America you can find the Andes mountains,
the Iguassu Falls, the Amazon river, the Southern glaciers,
and countless scenic spots along the coastline.

People work hard to make a living
for they arrived without any money or connections;
many made successes out of their businesses,
but there are also many who failed, and have nowhere to go.
They all would have left their homes far away
with the intentions to succeed,
but there are still those that struggle.
They strive so that they can eat and survive,
but at a time in the world when money has become the highest,
nothing can be done without it.
It is now held in higher regard than people
so it dictates people's happiness and sorrows,
although man existed long before there was money in the world.
If it is winter in Korea, it is summer here in South America,
and all of the beautiful nature here has grown and ripened.
It is also a place where day by day,
the people become more hard-hearted and pitiless,
but as if to mock man who is heartless,
nature continues to do its work silently.
It is man who reaps the benefits,
because the fruits of nature enable him to eat and survive.
Do we eat to live, or do we live to eat?
Such words arise from the weariness of life.
The purpose behind man's life is to become Truth
and he will be able to properly fulfill his role

when he becomes Truth and detaches himself from the material world.
What this means is when man changes from his greedy selfish mind,
when he no longer has the evil human mind,
his mind can become that of the whole,
and he can live for the whole.
That is, he will live for the people of the world,
and live to make the world a great place -
a place where the conceptions of *your* country and *my* country do not exist.
Namely, the world will become one;
it will become a paradise.
The best education is one that transforms false man into Truth
and when the world becomes a place where everyone lives as one,
it will be a great, great place to live.
It is a pity that even when the ultimate method exists -
one that can make the world a joyful place -
the people of the world live lives that place money over people.
Although there will surely come a time when the whole world will become true,
it is such a pity people are not putting in any effort to become true.
Having become Truth, I find it a shame, such a shame,
that man does not know he must go towards eternal life
and he continues to live holding onto the affairs of the world.
Although it is death if one does not become true,

a person who has not become true does not know he will die;
instead only those who have become true finds this pitiful.
While one chases money, life passes by and disappears.
Whether one earns money or not, it is all useless
because he ends up dying and is not able to live.

Ulleung Island

There is a small wooden boat floating beside the ship,
and on it, a poor fisherman is catching fish that are in season
to eke out a living for his family.
In order to catch even a few,
he needs to go far out into the open ocean.
The fisherman catches fish throughout the night,
while listening to the pounding of the waves against his boat.
The strong winds make for big waves, but despite them,
he continues to catch fish that can be readily caught in this type of weather.
He does not suffer from seasickness,
perhaps because he has been doing this for a long time.
When the horizon turns a reddish hue, he gathers in the nets,
and the cold morning air of the way back home
makes him forget his struggle with the waves.
His wife and children who have slept the whole night curled up like shrimps,
come out to greet him and help to unload the catch off the boat.

For the people of the fishing trade, the ocean is their life-line.
There have always been many widows near the ocean
because until even a few decades ago, many men died out at sea.
Many fishermen who were too poor to leave,
plied their trade fighting with the waves,
but most of their old wooden boats have now been replaced
with motored boats.
Although their work has become much easier,
they still live in fear of the waves.
A big passenger ship pulls in, sounding its foghorn,
and an eldest son who moved away from home
alights laden with presents.
Everyone greets him joyfully.
Ulleung Island has beautiful mountains
and lots of squid, being located in the Eastern Sea.
A truly beautiful island, with steep rocks near the shore
that have been shaped over thousands of years
by the pounding of the waves and rain.
There are lots of squid, cedar trees,
and wild herbs such as asters and lily leeks.
On the way from *Do-dong* to *Chun-bu*,
there is a waterfall and a mountain path,
that are too beautiful to describe with words.
The residents of this place make their living
by growing garlic, corn and potatoes,

raising cows and catching squid.

The water is pure, and the people of this island are gentle,

so the expressions on their faces are relatively open and bright.

In every valley, there is a fishing village,

and although in the past, they could only be reached on foot or by boat,

they can now be reached by car.

Many people have left, so the population has decreased.

The people of this place used to be generous and warm-hearted -

it is a shame that they do not live in the world.

A True Person Lives A True Life

To have life is to exist,
and it is to live life fulfilling one's role.
Man's role is to become a true person,
to become the salt and light of the true world.
One's role is to become a person who lives for the true world.
We must change from our self-centered lives
to a Truth-centered life.
We must build blessings in that world,
and amass fortunes in that world.
Only this is existence,
and only this is a true life.
Saving people is a blessing among blessings.
If many people are able to live, if all people are able to live,
wouldn't it be wonderful?
Only a person who knows the falseness of human life
and the falseness of everything man has, will live this way.
A person who has become true will live this way.

God Is Complete And Lives Forever - God Is A Person Who Does Not Have A False Self And Has Been Reborn As God

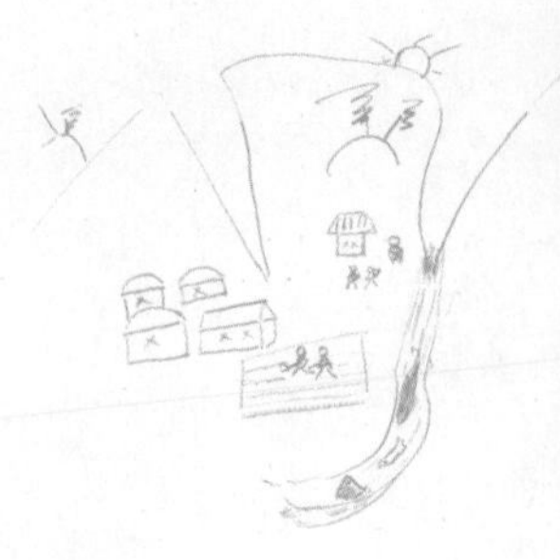

People live agonizing,
and carrying burdens in their mind.
The burdens of one's mind are the minds he himself has made;
they are the minds he has possessed.
When one lives with those minds,
he is uselessly busy and it brings suffering,
because he must live as the pictures, the illusions, order him to live.
Dear people,
a human lifetime has so many trials and tribulations,
and one who lives within them will find life tedious.
He who lives within them will live in suffering and burden.
There is nowhere for him to go, no matter how far he goes,
and nothing is achieved, no matter how much he tries or does achieve,
because it is a futile life that does not exist.
The creations of the world are born, exist, and live,
according to their conditions.
They are born by the mingling and coming together of various

things,
so *this* exists because *that* exists,
and *that* exists because *this* exists;
namely everything is born according to the harmony of heaven and earth.
If you look from the viewpoint of the origin,
everything is the embodiment of the origin,
and all things are the children of the origin.
The source of all creations is the origin;
the source of all creations is the original *Jung* and *Shin*.
People have no significance or meaning,
because they have made stories of the origin.
He who has returned to the origin, to Truth,
does not die, he is freedom and liberation itself,
free from all affairs of life.
The place of completeness where good and bad, hot and not hot,
existence and non-existence of human affairs do not exist;
the place that is beyond even life and death is the place of God,
where everything exists as they are eternally, of and by themselves.
Man can become God,
when his old self, his self that is a delusion completely dies.
Then only God remains,
and he can be reborn as God.
God who is complete is alive as *Jung* and *Shin*,
and when we are also reborn as this *Jung* and *Shin*

we can live as God in the land of God.

The land of God is completely free from human conceptions and habits;

it is freedom, liberation, and wisdom,

because one's self, the illusionary person, does not exist.

It is thus completion and the place free from human conceptions and habits.

The place of God is not a material place,

but it is the true metaphysical essence.

There is absolutely nothing, yet *Jung* and *Shin* exist there,

and to be resurrected and reborn as this *Jung* and *Shin*,

one must die completely.

It is a complete death only when his mind world and self is completely dead.

When one gets rid of himself completely,

the consciousness that does not die remains,

and when one gets rid of himself completely,

he can be born as this consciousness.

Then this heaven and earth is the world that has been born anew,

and this heaven and earth is paradise.

He will live forever without dying in this heaven and earth.

To be complete is to be without death,

and it is to be free from all intrusions.

The existence that exists of and by itself is the complete existence.

Man must be reborn and resurrected as this existence

and he must live in the land of this existence
if he is to be complete.
The present exists because of the past,
and the future exists because of the present.
The life that man lives is a human one,
and it is because he lives in a limited period of time,
that within it there is a past, present and future.
In the world of God, there is no past, present or future;
the past does not exist there because there is no picture world of the past,
and one is simply the mind of God, which just exists.
It exists just as it is.
This existence is always the mind of one,
and it is an existence that is alive.
The world of this existence has transcended time and space,
and although the world of this existence is alive,
it is not within life,
and it is not within its actions.
There is nothing lacking in this world,
and it is a place free from this and that.
It exists, but does not dwell in its existence,
and it is God because there is only the living mind of reality, and not illusions.
It is the God of wisdom.

Illusion And Reality

The place where the clouds stayed awhile,
where the wind stayed awhile,
the place where the clouds rested awhile,
and where the wind rested awhile,
is the origin.
All the countless events of human life are in the origin,
but man does not know the origin.
Time that flows by is in the origin,
as are countless events
filled with sighs, blame, love and hate.
But man does not know the origin
because he has separated from it
and he lives inside his own mind.
For what did he live his life having turned against the world?
What did he want to achieve,
that he turned his back on the world that is the origin?
Human mind does not exist in the origin.
It came into existence because of man's greed,

and his greed made him turn against the world.
But all he has done is take pictures of the world in his mind,
and he lives not in reality, but in an illusion, holding onto illusions.
It is something to be ashamed of.
All those who boast of how great they are
are living in a non-existent world,
but they do not know they are in such a world.
What man must achieve, and where man must go,
is the world of reality, the world of existence.
But man does not know where he must go,
or how to get there.
He only has the minds that he has eaten,
and he lives as a slave to those minds.
He does not know what is right and correct
because his mind is clouded by the minds he has taken in.
He does not know he is in a useless world,
he does not know what it is he has to do,
and he lives thinking the conceptions and habits of the minds he has
eaten are correct,
but they are only illusions of pictures taken.
Man is a ghost
because he lives inside an illusion where nothing is right.

Human Completion

The origin of completion is the sky before the sky,
that is, it is *Jung* and *Shin* - the origin of the Universe.
While it is true that all creations are complete,
it is also true that all creations and man can become complete
only when completion comes as a person.
People often believe that they themselves are buddhas,
but because they live in an illusionary picture world,
they are not buddhas, or saints,
but illusions and pictures.
When one completely dies and becomes the origin that is completion itself,
the complete person will make him complete
by resurrecting him and making him live in the land of completion.
To become a Buddha, one must completely die
for only then does that which is real remain,
and he must be born from it.
To be reborn, there must only be Truth, with none of one's false self remaining,

and he can only be born and live in that world if Truth gives him new birth.

Only that which is real can bring about human completion, and such is Truth;

only that which is real can save man in the real land.

Just as there are fertilized and unfertilized eggs,

there must be man's true self inside him

to become the Universe after he dies

and for his true self, who is God, to live.

Human completion is when one has a true soul resurrected within him,

and such a person is complete and Truth.

The Hungered Affairs of Human Life

Man lives out his lifetime running amok with hunger,
in the hungered affairs of human life.
Exhausted from hunger, he eventually collapses and dies.
It was a hunger that did not do or achieve anything,
a false and non-existent illusion.
The hunger burdened him and made him busy,
but nothing remains from it.
Only a person who has true energy, knows the futility of a hungered life,
and only he knows the true world.
Although hungered people have sung songs and told stories
of life being that of a weed, of a floating cloud,
of a bubble, of a spring-time dream,
they were just songs and stories of their hungered greed.
They did not truly know Truth.

Truth, Which Just Exists

Whether the wind blows, or the rain falls,
the mind that is true just exists.
Regardless of the water flowing by, or how the world changes,
the mind that is true just exists.
His mind just exists, even as he ages
and his forehead becomes lined along with the passage of time,
and his mind just exists, even when he dies.
There may be many things that happen in human life,
things that make him shout, or weep,
but his mind has departed from all regrets, all bitterness;
it has left all human matters.
Where is it, and where has it gone?
In the matters of human life,
one lives storing many regrets in his mind,
judging who is better than whom,
but such is the life of a floating cloud, and in it, no one is great.
There are only a lot of words,
and only in words is he great,

but nothing about him is actually great.
If one does not know that life is like a bubble that disappears,
it is because he himself is a bubble and he is not born in the world
and he does not live in it.
Man for whom there is no end no matter how far he goes and goes,
man who does not know where he must go,
only roams round and round inside his mind.
When Truth comes, without sound, smell or taste,
when Truth comes without fore-warning,
he will teach the ways of the world
and he will speak of the world.
But man who does not know the meaning or purpose of life
will not be able to see him or hear his words.

When I Began To Teach People

The train passes over the rails,
making a clickety-clackety noise as it rushes by.
It makes me think of those days of long ago,
when I could hear the far-off sounds of the train
in the early hours of the morning.
The noises of the *Kyungbu* railway may make
the people who live in the villages alongside it
want to leave and travel somewhere.
The many, many people who take the train
all have their own stories.
I once took a train during the saddest time of my life
and looked around to see if anyone was as sad as I was,
but other people were all slouched in their seats sleeping
and only I was sad.
Now as I look back at the events of that time,
when I was the saddest I had ever been,
I realize that for quite awhile I had forgotten them.
In my childhood and youth, and even as I grew older,

I lived without ever having laughed properly.
Why man had to die after living this way,
was a perpetual riddle in my mind.
In those days my mind held sighs and regrets,
and alcohol became my best companion.
It was my assignment of assignments,
to figure out where man comes from,
why he lives, and where he goes.
No one knew why I drank so much,
they only knew me as a person who drank a lot.
As we grew older my friends began to live lives
that revolved more and more around the events of each day,
but I cared more for others than myself.
As time went on, everyone I knew became busier and busier,
chased by the circumstances of their daily lives,
because they lived trying to protect themselves inside their self-centered lives.
On the other hand, I wished for others' success,
because I doubted if there was any meaning or significance
in a life where only I lived well.
While many people were living only for their own sake,
I sacrificed my personal life, and tried in my own way to live for others.
I sometimes wondered why in a world where everyone was created together,
only some people became saints,

while I remained an ordinary person.
The past saints were chosen by heaven,
to prophesy the coming of a real saint at a certain time in the world.
All scriptures are indeed stories of Truth,
but furthermore, they speak of a time when man will become complete;
they speak of the age of human completion.
Only when a complete person comes to the world,
can man become complete.
Completion is the Universe itself,
and a complete person is he who comes to the world as such.
Man believes he lives by his own will,
but only after he has matured
will he know he lives not by his own will,
but by the will of the world.
He will also know the ways of the world, afterwards,
when he has matured,
and he will become one with the world.
The world just existed,
but during the time of immaturity,
I too lived like a vagabond,
endlessly rushed and busy;
rushing here and there but without actually achieving anything,
like a rat inside a well.
It makes me dizzy to think of that time,

when I nearly ended up dying,
and now, it seems like a dream.
Although in the human world,
there is nothing great about me or anything I did,
I have shed light on the ways of the world
which was a constant enigma,
so I have in a way, achieved my will.
Although people may all look the same,
a person who has Truth in him,
a person who has become complete,
is not human, but God.
Although I did not even dream of it,
I have come to the human world as the master of the world,
and I am teaching man how to become complete.
The method for man to become complete is
to discard one's false body and mind
and to be reborn with the real body and mind.
It seems this method is popular.
For over ten years, many people have become free and liberated,
and they have gone to eternal heaven,
so I feel that I have done my work in the world.

Man's Destiny

The wind and clouds are sleeping,
and only man who does not have anywhere to go,
is uselessly busy without doing his work.
The world is hectic because people are hectic.
Great nature just exists, and all creations just live,
and only man, who does not achieve anything,
is bewilderedly living in the illusionary world inside his mind,
living according to the pictures that have been taken,
without freedom, according to what the pictures have scripted.
By himself, he has trapped himself in the ground.
The ground is the illusionary world, and he lives in it.
Thus, he lives with the suffering and burden of the world of hell.
However, that world is an illusion,
because it does not exist in the world of reality.
He who is born on the ground, lives on the ground -
this means such a person is living in hell,
because he is born on the ground and lives in the tunnel of his
mind.

The expression, he who is born in heaven lives in heaven,
means such a person lives with the mind of reality that is Truth and heaven,
because he is born in heaven, outside the tunnel of the mind;
he is one with the whole world,
and he lives in heaven, the land of Truth.
Falseness becoming Truth is completion,
and when all falseness disappears, Truth remains.
When one's false body and mind disappears, that which is real remains.
When man is born as what is real,
he will do what he needs to do - he will do his work -
and he will become complete.
Man can become complete when he discards his self that is false
and is reborn as a real person.
One must live eternally while he is alive,
and one must go to heaven, while he is still alive.
There are so many people living in the world,
but there is no righteous person who has been born in heaven,
thus man does not know he is dead,
and he does not know what it is to live.
No one knows the world they live in is an illusion.
A true person knows what it is to be dead and what it is to live.
He who knows is he who has been born and who lives in the world -
the land of Truth.

To know is to know the ways of the world;
to know the ways of the world is to know the origin of the world,
it is to know that existence and non-existence of the world is one,
and it is to know the significance of being born, dying and living.
Knowing the ways of the true world is real knowledge and wisdom.
The source - the origin of the world - must come as a person
in order for the world to be saved.
This is because such a person is the master of the world,
and because he is able to save and kill,
and to make things exist and disappear.
This is the power over life and death.

Let's Live A Lifetime Of The World

Man believes that life is to live with the human body;
such a life is a human life;
a human lifetime.
But a true life is to become Truth,
and to become eternal and invincible God.
Man can live forever when he is reborn with the consciousness of Truth, the origin.
There are countless stories in human life because one's mind world exists,
but he who has become one with great nature that is God, Buddha and Allah,
does not have a mind world, and just lives having become one with nature.
Dear people,
do not live a human lifetime -
let's live a lifetime of the world.
While living in the world,
people most cherish their own selves,

and they live for themselves.
They do not know how to cherish and love their true selves
and instead cherish and love their false selves.
Man is so infinitely foolish.
If man destroys his fixed frame of mind - his mind world -
and is reborn in the true world that is Truth,
he will become complete.
He must throw away his false self that he cherishes and loves,
in order to be born as a true person.
The person that is reborn is God,
and he is without death.
Oh people, the world is true and Truth,
but you are not able to live in the world,
and you live trapped in your own mind,
and although you mistakenly believe you live in the world,
you are in the world of your own mind,
made by taking pictures of the world.
This mind is not real but a picture,
and the world that is false and not real, only has falseness within,
so there is suffering and burden.
The real world is a place free from all greed.
It is free of and by itself, and although it exists of and by itself,
this thought, this mind, does not exist;
such a place is the place of he who has become Truth.
God has absolutely no minds,

and yet, God knows everything.

God is an entity that exists of and by itself,

free from all human minds;

God is wisdom itself.

Wisdom is to know the principles of the world's origin,

to know that the world's existence and non-existence is one,

to know the true meaning of living and dying,

and to know everything in the world from the viewpoint of God.

Such is wisdom.

Wisdom is to see and know everything from God's point of view.

Man Lives According To What He Has In His Mind

The flowing river lives by flowing
and time that flows cannot be seen,
but it exists in the mind world of man.
A noble person is none other than a person who has been born as Truth;
and such a person is the temple of Truth.
A person who has been born as Truth inside himself is complete.
What flies, flies because of the conditions that allow it to fly,
while what crawls, crawls because of the conditions that allow it to crawl.
What walks with four legs does so because it has four legs,
while what walks with two, does so because it is two-legged.
All things in existence exist as Truth but people can know this
only when they are born in the true world.
Everything in one's mind, all fantasies
are drawn by illusions of the mind;
it is a wise person that knows that they are seeds of illusion.
All the various things that exist,

all the various life-forms there are,
are all Truth.
They are born according to the conditions of the world,
and live according to their conditions,
but only he who has become the origin knows this.
In order to know that his countless futile thoughts and delusions
are non-existent and without meaning,
one must go to the origin.
The many stories people feel unable to tell
are all of the human mind;
however the origin knows
one just lives, and just exists,
which can only be known by the origin that is complete.
He who has gone to the origin knows
the many stories of the world are false
but all those in the human mind world do not.
Man who lives with time has many regrets and much to say,
but regardless of what he says, his words are all the chattering of illusions;
he lives an illusionary life.
However the place that has transcended time,
the place beyond the various things of the human world:
good, bad, likes, dislikes, right, wrong, hot, cold,
knowledge, ignorance, death, life,
boring, interesting, living, dying, sin and karma,

virtue, goodness, penance and pleasure;
the place that is free from all human conceptions and habits
which arise from birth and death,
is the origin that is the land of God.
He who is born in this place of the origin has escaped
from the fixed frames of all human conceptions and habits.
It is freedom and liberation;
free and liberated because one's self does not exist.
Resurrected as Truth because his self does not exist,
there is no self whatsoever,
and he is free and liberated because he is free from everything.
Like God, he just exists of and by himself,
so he is eternal and invincible.
He is not restricted or restrained by anything, so he is free.
He is free because there is no judgment or discrimination.
He is free because he is free from birth, death, ageing and sickness.
He is free because he is free from joy, anger, sorrow and pleasure.
His body is a temple,
because the consciousness within is the consciousness of the world.
He is a temple,
because the whole world exists within him.
Man lives according to what he has in his mind.
He who has Truth in his mind will live born in the land of Truth,
while he who has illusions in his mind, will live in an illusion.
He who has been born in heaven will live in heaven,

and he who has been born on earth will live on earth.
He who has been born on the earth -
he who has the pictures of the earth -
will live in a picture,
while he who has been born in heaven that is the origin and source
will be born and live in the kingdom of heaven.
He who has the world in his mind,
will live with the world.

It Is Okay For A Ghost To Have Nothing

1. Money 1. Love 1. Fame 1. Death
1. Family 1. Pride 1. The World

Is it ok not to have money? OK
Is it ok not to have love? OK
Is it ok not to have fame? OK
Is it ok not to have family? OK
Is it ok not to have pride? OK
Is it OK for you to die? OK
Is it OK for the world not to exist? OK

The mind of acceptance is the mind of God.
For a ghost, nothing is OK,
but the mind of God is the mind of acceptance -
everything is OK.
It is OK for a ghost not to have money.
It is OK for a ghost not to have love.
It is OK for a ghost not to have fame.

It is OK for a ghost not to have family.

It is OK for a ghost to have his pride hurt and to not have any pride.

It is OK for a ghost to die.

It is OK for a ghost not to have the world.

God

God is the origin: the metaphysical real substance without form.
The source of the Universe consists of *Jung* and *Shin*.
This existence is not material,
but it is a self-existing existence.
Man only knows that which is already in his mind,
so he can know this existence
only when it exists in him;
and only to the extent it exists in him.
Completion is a person who has been born as this existence itself,
and only such a person can properly know this existence.
Although this existence is alive, it does not have the mind of being alive;
it is the place of mind that has transcended everything:
it has transcended all knowledge,
and it is beyond everything of the human world.
What exists in the world is man's mind, his conceptions and habits;
and what exists in the human mind are all illusions.
The place of God where man's mind, his conceptions and habits

have departed,
is a complete and perfect place.
God does not dwell in existence,
though the things of the world may exist,
and it is completely free and liberated
because even the mind of existence does not exist.
It lives, and yet, it is not within life,
it is an existence that just exists -
an eternally living immortal.

Let's Go, Let's Go

Leave behind your regrets and everything of human life,
and let's go to the eternal and invincible land of God.
Discard, and discard again, all the many things you had in the human world -
those things that have become greed in your mind -
and be reborn in the world where you do not exist,
in the world where there is only Truth.
Only when you are born as a new person,
with a new body and mind,
are you an eternally living immortal.
Then, there is nothing of the human world -
aging, sickness, birth, life,
joy, sorrow, anger and happiness,
the seven emotions and five desires -
these do not exist there.
Though you exist, you are not within existence,
and though you live, you are not within life.
None of the many human conceptions exist -

discriminating between this and that.

God's mind is one that has departed from all knowing,

it is the mind of non-existence.

That which is non-existent, exists,

but it is said to be non-existent because its mind is complete.

Heaven, which we have only heard of, is the land

where those who become the consciousness of the great Universe

have gone, and it is where they dwell.

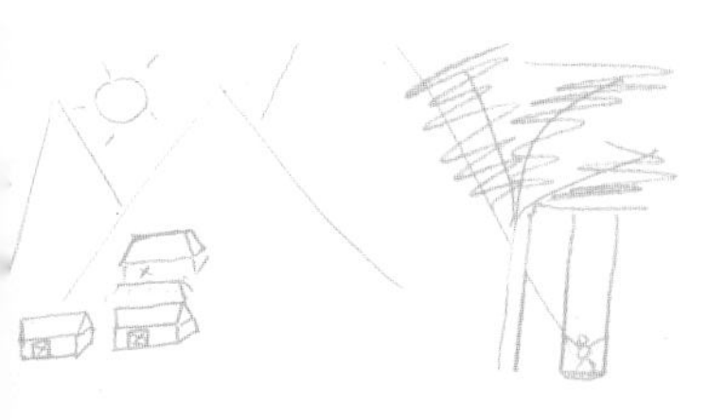

The Land Of Human Completion

Indelible events were all vain illusions,
and time that passes is also a delusion.
The countless times of struggle
when I did not know where to go,
or what it was that I wanted to find,
were all such foolishness I do not even remember them.
All people - the silent and the noisy -
have followed the passage of time
and what remains in my mind are all illusions and delusions.
What was told to people as if it was the way,
only made them wander further from the true path
in the illusionary world without meaning or significance.
All the thoughts and actions that went round and round in my head
like a squirrel running endlessly in its wheel with no destination,
were vain delusions; they were false and useless deeds.
Inside my mind of greed, my false self existed and thus,
I had pride.
I had anguish.

I had money.
I had family.
I had fame and love.
When that self completely died and those minds were gone,
my whole mind disappeared.
Time that passes disappeared,
the places I needed to go disappeared,
and the numerous things I needed to achieve disappeared.
Money, love, pride, fame and family, my false self
all disappeared.
Although my false self no longer exists,
I am born in the world of God beyond my mind world;
from my mind world, it is now the world of God.
God, which we have only heard of, is freedom and liberation;
free from everything in the world.
It is freedom because the world that disappears with time
and the flowing river have gone;
even time no longer exists.
Now there is only time that just simply exists,
not the time that passes.
Bitterness and regrets arising from failure to achieve has gone,
so it is *haewonsangsaeng* -
the resolution and dissipation of all regrets, and living for others.
To the people who live in this false world,
if you know that this body and mind is false,

you can know everything is all your fault,
and that your illusionary self deserves to die.
For what reason does an illusion have
bitterness, regrets, family, money, love, fame and pride?
Everything in the world is inside the mind that your illusionary self made;
this is this, that is that, right and wrong, countless doubts and suspicions
all exist inside the dark tomb that is your mind world.
This world is false and if this world and your self do not exist,
there is the true world.
If you are born in the true world,
you have achieved everything;
you are a perfect and complete existence.
When there is absolutely nothing in the clear sky,
but heaven and earth has been born inside man's consciousness
and he lives as the master of heaven and earth, it is heaven.
A life with meaning is a life that is lived
when one's mind has become heaven and earth -
it is a life lived born within this heaven and earth.

A Person Who Has Not Prepared Himself For Where He Needs To Go

Man holds onto countless past events as he ages,
and he eventually dies inside the formless world of those events,
reminiscing about those events of the past.
The world made by one's non-existent self is a world of illusion.
Man, who does not know the true will or purpose,
is ignorant of where he must go,
and where he should truly live.
Neither does he know what he must do while he is alive.
He does not adjust himself to the world,
and instead tries to make the world adapt to him
but the pains he took to do this are the only result.
Man lives within the passing time without reason or meaning,
and he wastes away the years inside an illusionary world,
only to end up dying.
Man, who has nowhere to go, does not know anything.
He does not prepare for where he must go,
and he continues to live in the world of ghosts.
All of the countless stories of past events

are about the futile affairs of life,
which do not remain in the world.
There is nothing that remains in the human world,
everything is a false dream after they have passed,
and because they all disappear, the human world is utterly futile.
Man, who has nowhere to go, walks to and fro
because he does not know where he should go,
and the path he does end up traveling is a false one;
on it, he does and achieves nothing.
The wisest person is he who makes sure he remains in the world;
he can remain forever if he is reborn as the body and mind of Truth.
One can live only when his false body and mind - his very self - disappears,
and when he returns to Truth itself, and is reborn in that land.
Returning to the origin is Truth.
Cleansing the human body and mind,
in other words, getting rid of one's body and mind
which exist in his mind so that only the origin remains,
and being reborn from that origin
is the way man can live forever.

Acceptance

The greatest person in the world is he who is able to accept.

God has transcended everything;

therefore, he is able to accept everything.

To accept is to have something, but to not be within what one has.

The righteous way or method: correct will: true will: the will of Truth.

Words That Are Of Use

The world is a noisy place, full of many words,
and although much has been said,
none of it is of any use.
Useful words are the words of Truth;
words that save people.
Useful words are living words.
Living words must have life,
and living words are words of life.
In conclusion, they are useful words.
Words that have life, and are living, are of use;
they are the words of a person who is alive,
they are words that are themselves living.
Words of use are the words of Truth,
and words of use are the words of life.

The Mind of Universal Order

The reason man believes his past memories are beautiful
is only the memories remain in his mind,
and he does not have the emotions behind those memories.
He misses his childhood because when he is young,
his mind is yet uncluttered by many different minds.
In the tumultuous human mind,
the past has transformed into longing.
The world is all inside man's mind,
but the human mind wants to do just as it wishes,
and the world does not move according to it.
He whose mind has become the world
lives adjusting to the movements of the world,
with the mind of universal order.
He lives without the mind of suffering.
It is because man is foolish that he lives with suffering,
and because he is foolish, he lives with delusions,
and because he is foolish, he lives with heavy burdens.

Let's Return To Nature

Man is not in the world,
he is inside his mind,
and he speaks, acts and lives within his mind.
All those who raucously claimed life is
non-existent, futile, and like a weed,
have disappeared from the world.

There is an old grandma, who in the past believed her life,
of having children and making a home, to be a happy one.
But all her relationships scattered over time,
and now, having become an old grandma,
she is alone, gnawing and eating something with her toothless
gums.
The members of her once big family have all gone somewhere,
and the masters of that time have gone to the next world.
She now lives in the old house of the past alone
and her days left in the world are also numbered.
While the many trials and tribulations have disappeared with time,

all the stories of her life remain inside her mind,
and she speaks, again and again, of the past.
In that world, in which she does not know where to go,
the world in which there is nowhere to go,
she is so ignorant that she does not worry;
she believes when she dies
she will live once more with her husband and ancestors.
She is particularly kinder and more loving to the descendants
whom she believes will perform her ancestral rites,
in order that she may come and eat the ceremonial food they offer.

The people of the world who live a human life
do not know where to go, or how they live.
Countless stories of life after death have been passed down through
the ages
but no one knows whether they are right or wrong.
Seen from the world, everyone who has gone on to the next world
has become nature; they have returned to the origin.
Man can live in paradise without dying,
only when the master of the origin gives him new birth
in the land of the origin that is without death.
But man can only know such ways of the world,
he can only know the afterworld, after he has died.
Dear people,
discard all worries, anxieties, all human affairs of sorrow,

and when your life is at an end, return back to nature
for only nature that originally exists, when you do not exist, must
remain.
He who lives in his own world,
lives in the world of hell
and hell is a world that does not exist.
It is a false world.
Let's be born in the true world.
Let's die completely so that only nature remains,
and in nature, let's be reborn.

In Order To Go To The True World

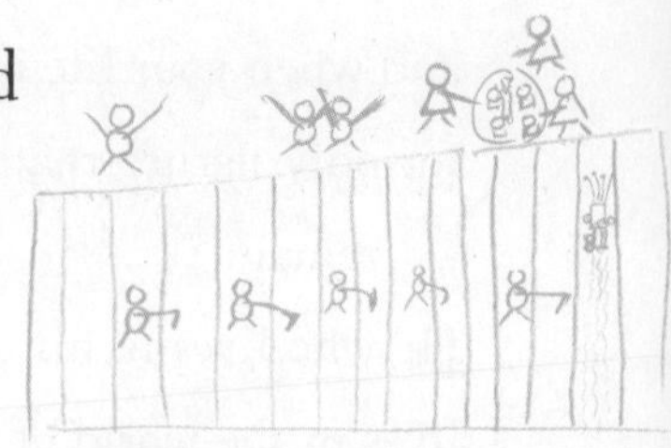

I can hear birdsong -
there are birds even in this bleak desert,
as well as snakes, deer, squirrels and mice.
It does not rain, so the trees are alive but tough,
changed into trees of thorns.
Near the spring, the trees and grass have grown as much
as they have had water to drink.
People live in the desert because it is dry and the climate is good,
particularly for old people who suffer from the cold or neuralgia.
Throughout the long ages, everything that has lived
have all disappeared, as have their forms;
they have returned to nature that is the origin.
Nature came into creation because within it
there exists a consciousness - the original foundation.
The master of the original foundation must come as a person
if all creations of the world and people
are to be taken to the land of the original foundation.
The whole world can be saved,

when everything in the world is destroyed and eliminated
and only the original foundation remains.
And when the master of the original foundation exists in one's mind,
all creations - the world - are resurrected
and can be reborn as the substance of the original foundation.
Man lives in his own mind and cannot reach the original foundation
because his consciousness is dead;
this state is in itself an illusion and hell.
He lives in his mind world
and within it,
he continuously goes through the cycle of birth and death;
this is suffering and burden.
If this mind world and his self living in it disappears,
he can see the original foundation while he is living,
and he can get there.
Man can live in the land of the original foundation,
only when the master of the original foundation allows him to live.
What this means is that a Savior must come,
in order for the world to be saved.
Rebirth and resurrection is to be reborn and resurrected
as the Soul whose substance is Truth;
for only this is true rebirth and true resurrection.
Man must go to the land of Truth that is inside his mind
if he is to be born in the world,
and he must be reborn in this land of Truth inside his mind.

The trees in the mountains may grow old and die,
disappear after crumbling into many pieces,
but the Universe remains.
In the same way, even if the whole world disappears, the Universe still exists.
Only when man is reborn as the substance of the original foundation of all creation can he become an eternally living immortal,
and when he exists in the land of Truth inside him,
he will never die.
When a person has become reborn while he is living in the true land within him, his body becomes a temple.
His true self lives within it so he does not die.
None of the creations in the world have any minds,
and thus they return to nature,
but because man lives within his mind,
he cannot return to nature that is Truth.
He lives in his delusional mind, suffering and burdened -
this is what hell is.
Heaven is the world that exists outside one's self and his mind world.
When one's mind world and self do not exist,
and he returns to the true world,
the master of the true world must resurrect him in that place
and allow him to live there;
only then can he actually live in that land.

The Principles Of The True World

There is a world without any clouds.
Countless things may come and go,
but they are created and they disappear according to the conditions that arise from the foundation of the origin.
All things are created because God exists amidst absolute nothingness,
and because this existence is alive,
it is said to be holy, or divine.
The original foundation is the origin of all creation,
and all creations are also this existence itself.
The forms of all creations are the appearance of the original foundation.
It is omnipotent because all sorts of things are created through the conditions that exist.
Seeing and knowing things from the viewpoint of the original foundation - the viewpoint of God - is omniscience.
In other words, omniscience is seeing and knowing things from the viewpoint of Truth.

The original foundation is the mother and father of all creations that have form.
All creations that have come into being in the world
will one day return to the original foundation;
this is nature's flow, it is the way of nature.
Nature's flow, or universal order, is the way of nature.
The way of nature is Truth,
and to be born and die is the way of nature;
but only a person who has gone to the original foundation can know this.
When the master of the original foundation comes as a person,
all things in the world can be saved,
and they can be saved for all eternity.
The true world exists within the master's mind,
so only when the master commands it to live can it exist.
What exists in man's mind disappears when man disappears;
and at that time only great nature, the original foundation, remains.
A person who is resurrected there lives.
Heaven is inside man's mind
and only he whose mind has become the original foundation will live;
without being resurrected as the body and mind of the original foundation,
no one can live.
He who claims that his self has become Truth,

has a self, so he is not Truth, and he cannot be born as Truth.
Only the master of the original foundation can resurrect him
and allow him to live in the land of Truth.
The Creator of all creations is the original foundation,
and the creation of the Souls of all things is done by the person
who is the master of the original foundation.
All creations are born and exist in the world
for a reason and a purpose:
to be reborn in the original foundation.
However not all people can live -
those who do not go to the original foundation
cannot live.

Confirmation Questions

Koans

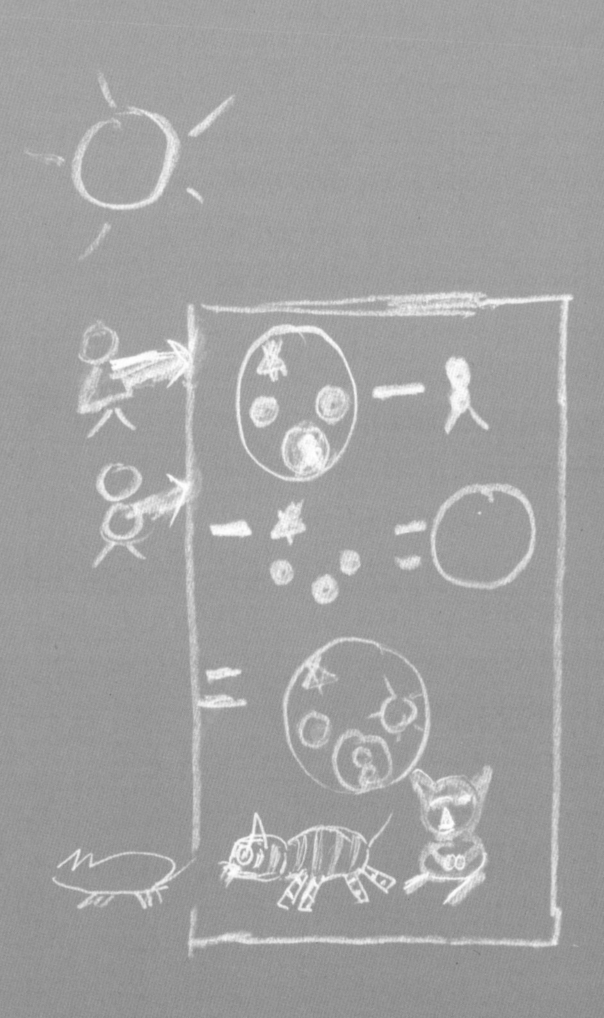

Confirmation Questions
Koans

1. The source of wisdom is knowing God. Why must one know God in order to have wisdom?
2. People do not know when Truth has come to the world - why is this?
3. Why is it that people do not know anything?
4. What will Truth do when it comes to the world?
5. What kind of actions will Truth show us?
6. Why are people unable to live?
7. Why are people illusions?
8. Why are people unable to die?
9. Who can make one into Truth? Why is it only Truth can do this?
10. Where do people go after they die?
11. Do heaven and hell exist or not?
12. What is the existence that sees, smells, hears, speaks and feels?
13. What kind of work does the Great Teacher do?
14. What is salvation? What is a Savior?
15. Why must one believe in Jesus in order to be saved?
16. Can one be saved if he does Maum Meditation?
17. Why is Truth free of sin and karma?
18. Which religion, which place is Truth?

19. With what kind of mentality must one do *dō* (Truth)?
20. God exists of and by himself but what does "of and by himself" mean?
21. How does God exist, and how does he live forever?
22. What is the prerequisite condition for the way to live eternally?
23. What is the time of completion?
24. How big is Truth?
25. How did the world become complete?
26. Why must one go to heaven while he is living?
27. What is sin and karma?
28. What is Truth?
29. Where do ghosts live?
30. Why hasn't one become Truth?
31. Why can illusions be seen?
32. How can one know whether he is alive or dead?
33. What is it to be possessed by a ghost?
34. What does "he who is born on earth lives on earth, and he who is born in heaven lives in heaven" mean?
35. What does Truth look like?
36. Why do people bear burden and suffering?
37. Why is it Truth does not burn even when in the hottest possible fire?
38. What does God dislike the most?
39. What kind of a person resembles heaven?
40. What is creation?
41. How does creation happen?
42. Who brings about creation?
43. Why is man false even though he speaks and moves?

Maum Meditation Centers
Location and Contact Details

Please visit www.maum.org for a full list of addresses, phone and fax numbers, as well as the locations and contact details of over 240 South Korean regional centers.

[South Korea]
Nonsan Main Center
82-41-731-1114

[U.S.A.]
AK
Anchorage
1-907-865-5954
CA
Berkeley
1-510-526-5121
Diamond Bar
1-909-861-6888
Irvine
1-949-502-5337
L.A. (Downtown)
1-213-484-9888
L.A. (Koreatown)
1-213-908-5151
Long Beach
1-562-900-5585
Orange
1-714-521-0325
San Diego
1-858-886-7363
San Fernando Valley
1-818-831-9888
San Francisco
1-650-301-3012
San Jose
1-408-615-0435
CO
Denver
1-303-481-8844
FL
Miami
1-954-379-6394
GA
Atlanta
1-678-683-4677
Smyrna
1-678-608-7271
HI
Honolulu
1-808-533-2875
IL
Chicago
1-888-979-6286
MA
Boston
1-617-272-6358
MD
Ellicott City
1-410-730-6604
NC
Raleigh
1-919-771-3808
NJ
Palisades Park
1-201-592-9988
Teaneck
1-201-801-0011
NV
Las Vegas
1-702-254-5484
NY
Bayside
1-718-225-3472
Flushing
1-718-353-6678
Manhattan
1-212-510-7052
Plainview
1-516-644-5231
PA
Elkins Park
1-215-366-1023
TX
Austin
1-512-585-6987
Dallas
1-469-522-1229
Houston
1-832-541-3523
North Richland Hills
1-214-801-1945
Plano
1-972-599-1623
VA
Annandale
1-703-354-8071
Centreville
1-703-815-2075
WA
Federal Way
1-253-520-2080
Lynnwood
1-425-336-0754

[Argentina]
Almagro
54-11-4862-5691
Flores
54-11-4633-6598
Floresta
54-11-3533-7544

[Australia]
Perth (Mandurah)
61-8-9586-2070
Perth (Vic Park)
61-8-9355-4114
Sydney
61-2-9804-6340

[Brazil]
Brasilia
55-61-3877-7420
Lindoia
55-19-3824-5842
Sao Paulo
55-11-3326-0656

[Cambodia]
Phnom Penh
855-78-901-434

[Canada]
Mississauga
1-289-232-3776
Montreal
1-514-507-7659
Toronto
1-416-730-1949
Vancouver
1-604-516-0709

[Chile]
Santiago
56-2-813-9657

[Colombia]
Bogota
57-1-487-4680

[England]
London
44-208-715-1601

[France]
Paris
33-1-4766-2997

[Germany]
Berlin
49-30-2100-5344

[Guatemala]
Guatemala City
502-2360-6081

[Hong Kong]
852-2572-0107

[Hungary]
Budapest
36-1-950-9974

[India]
Gurgaon
91-97178-63915

[Indonesia]
Tangerang
62-21-5421-1699

[Italy]
Genova
39-349-364-2607
Milan
39-2-3940-0932

[Japan]
Fukuoka
81-92-406-7588
Kyoto
81-75-708-2302
Osaka
81-6-6777-7312
Saitama (Omiya)
81-48-729-5787
Sendai
81-227-629-462
Tokyo (Machiya)
81-3-6806-6898
Tokyo (Shinjuku)
81-3-3356-1810
Yokohama
81-45-228-9926

[Kazakhstan]
Almaty
7-775-651-98-34

[Kenya]
Nairobi
254-20-520-3346

[Madagascar]
Antananarivo
261-34-9120-308

[Malaysia]
Johor Bahru
60-7-361-4900
Kuala Lumpur
60-12-920-2792

[Mexico]
Mexico City
52-55-5533-3925
Tijuana
52-664-380-8109

[Myanmar]
Yangon
95-94-2113-9996

[New Zealand]
Auckland
64-9-480-7245
Christchurch
64-3-358-7247

[Paraguay]
Asuncion
595-21-234-237

[Philippines]
Clark
63-45-624-7858
Manila
63-2-687-1294

[Russia]
Moscow
7-495-331-0660

[Singapore]
Marine Parade
65-6440-0323
Tanjong Pagar
65-6222-4171

[South Africa]
Pretoria
27-12-991-4986

[Sweden]
Stockholm
46-76-804-6806

[Taiwan]
Taipei
886-989-763-445

[Thailand]
Bangkok
66-2-261-2570

[Vietnam]
Hanoi
84-169-698-1968
Ho Chi Minh City
84-8-5412-4989